D1602755

Seal of the State of South Carolina

CHRONOLOGY AND DOCUMENTARY HANDBOOK OF THE STATE OF
SOUTH CAROLINA

ROBERT I. VEXLER

State Editor

WILLIAM F. SWINDLER

Series Editor

1978 OCEANA PUBLICATIONS, INC./Dobbs Ferry, New York

Library of Congress Cataloging in Publication Data

Main entry under title:

Chronology and documentary handbook of the State of
    South Carolina.

    (Chronologies and documentary handbooks of the
States; 40)
        Bibliography: p.
        Includes index.
        SUMMARY: A history of South Carolina in chronological
format, with supporting documents, biographical outlines
of chief State politicians and prominent personalities,
and a name index.
        1. South Carolina—History—Chronology.
2. South Carolina—Biography.   3. South Carolina—
History—Sources.   [1. South Carolina—History]
I. Vexler, Robert I.   II. Series.
F269.5.C48   975.7'002'02   78-26305
ISBN 0-379-16165-6

Manufactured in the United States of America

TABLE OF CONTENTS

ACKNOWLEDGMENT

Special recognition should be accorded Melvin Hecker, whose research has made a valuable contribution to this volume.

Thanks to my wife, Francine, in appreciation of her help in the preparation of this work.

Thanks also to my children, David and Melissa, without whose patience and understanding I would have been unable to devote the considerable time necessary for completing the state chronology series.

I also wish to acknowledge the scholarly research grant given to me by Pace University. This greatly eased the technical preparation of this work.

Robert I. Vexler
Pace University

INTRODUCTION

This projected series of *Chronologies and Documentary Handbooks of the States* will ultimately comprise fifty separate volumes—one for each of the states of the Union. Each volume is intended to provide a concise ready reference to basic data on the state, and to serve as a starting point for more extended study as the individual user may require. Hopefully, it will be a guidebook for a better informed citizenry - students, civic and service organizations, professional and business personnel, and others.

The editorial plan for the *Handbook* series falls into six divisions: (1) a chronology of selected events in the history of the state; (2) a short biographical directory of the principal public officials, e.g., governors, Senators and Representatives; (3) a short biographical directory of prominent personalities of the state (for most states); (4) the first state constitution; (5) the text of some representative documents illustrating main currents in the political, economic, social or cultural history of the state; and (6) a selected bibliography for those seeking further or more detailed information. Most of the data found in the present volume, in fact, have been taken from one or another of these references.

The current constitutions of all fifty states, as well as the federal Constitution, are regularly kept up to date in the definitive collection maintained by the Legislative Drafting Research of Columbia University and published by the publisher of the present series of *Handbooks*. These texts are available in most major libraries under the title, *Constitutions of the United States: National and State,* in two volumes, with a companion volume, the *Index Digest of State Constitutions.*

Finally, the complete collection of documents illustrative of the constitutional development of each state, from colonial or territorial status up to the current constitution as found in the Columbia University collection, is being prepared for publication in a multi-volume series by the present series editor. Whereas the present series of *Handbooks* is intended for a wide range of interested citizens, the series of annotated constitutional materials in the volumes of *Sources and Documents of U.S. Constitutions* is primarily for the specialist in government, history or law. This is not to suggest that the general citizenry may not profit equally from referring to these materials; rather it points up the separate purpose of the *Handbooks*, which is to guide the user of these and other sources of authoritative information with which he may systematically enrich his knowledge of this state and its place in the American Union.

William J. Swindler
John Marshall Professor of Law
College of William and Mary
Series Editor

Robert I. Vexler
Associate Professor of History
Pace University
Series Associate Editor

Animis Opibusque Parati/
Prepared in Mind and Resources
Dum Spiro Spero/
While I Breathe, I Hope

State Motto

CHRONOLOGY

1520	Spaniards from Cuba were the first Europeans to visit the coast of South Carolina.
1521	Francisco de Gordillo explored the South Carolina coast for Spain.
1526-27	Lucas Vásquez de Ayllón attempted unsuccessfully to found a colony near present-day Georgetown for the Spaniards.
1526-64	Jean Ribaut led some French Huguenots in an unsuccessful attempt to found a settlement on Parris Island near the mouth of the Broad River.
1629	King Charles I of England granted all land lying between the 31st and 36th parallels to his attorney general Sir Robert Heath.
1663	King Charles II of England granted the territory between the 31st and 36th parallels to the Earl of Clarendon and six other favorites.
1665	King Charles II granted a second charter for Carolina extending it to the area between 29° and 36°30'.
1669	The Fundamental Constitution, written by John Locke and Lord Ashley, was adopted by the proprietary board. It presented a feudal system of government.
1670	Estimated population: 200
	March. Joseph West led a party of colonists who established a settlement at Port Royal Sound.
	April. The settlers moved north to the Ashley River at Albemarle Sound to a spot which later became Old Charles Town. The settlement moved again in 1680 to the point where the Ashley and Cooper Rivers meet.
	William Sayle became governor of the colony and served until 1671.
1671	The Kussos Indians were defeated in the area of Charles Town.

1

Joseph West became governor of South Carolina. He served in the post until 1672.

1672   Sir John Yeamans became governor. He served in the office until 1674.

1674   May. Dr. Henry Woodward received a commission to open up trade with the Westo Indians, east of the lower Savannah River. He was to trade in furs, deer hides and slaves.

Joseph West again became governor of the colony and remained in the office until 1682

1680   Estimated population: 1,200

April. The Westo Indians began an uprising which was crushed by the end of the year.

1682   Joseph Morton became governor. He served in the office until 1684

1684   Richard Kyrle became governor of South Carolina and served for a brief period.

Robert Quarry was chosen governor of the colony by the Council. He served in the post until 1685.

1685   Joseph West again served as governor of the colony briefly.

Joseph Morton became governor again. He remained in the office until 1686.

Berkley, Colleton and Craven Counties were created.

1686   James Colleton became governor of South Carolina and served in the post until 1690.

1690   Estimated population: 3,900.

October. Seth Southell, governor of Albemarle in the north removed Governor Colleton and took over the government. Southell served in the gubernatorial office until 1692.

1692   The colonial legislature was divided into
            two houses.

            Philip Ludwell became governor of the colony
            and served in the post until 1693.

1693   The house of commons, elected by the people,
            gained the right to initiate legislation.

            Thomas Smith **became** governor. He served
            in the office until 1694.

1694   Joseph Blake was chosen governor by the
            Council. He served in the office until
            1700.

1697   A smallpox epidemic broke out in Charles-
            ton.

1699   The royal collector of customs arrived
            in South Carolina.

1700   Estimated population: 5,704

            James Moore was selected governor by the
            Council and served in the post until 1702.

1702   Sir Nathaniel Johnson became governor of
            the colony. He served in the post until
            1710.

1706   November 30. The Church of England was
            established in the colony.

            A French-Spanish attack on Charles Town was
            defeated.

1710   Estimated population: 10,883.

            Edward Tinton served as governor for a
            brief period.

            Robert Gibbes was chosen governor by the
            Council. He served in the post until
            1711.

1711   The settlers began a war with the Tuscarora
            Indians which lasted until 1713.

            Charles Craven became governor and continued
            in the office until 1716.

1712   May 9. The Territory was divided into
            North and South Carolina, each having
            its own governor.

1715   Approximately 400 settlers were killed in a
            war with the Yamassee Indians.

1716   January. The settlers defeated the Yamas-
            sees.

            Robert Daniel became deputy governor of
            the colony and served in the office until
            1717.

1717   Robert Johnson became governor of South
            Carolina and remained in the office until
            1719.

1718   Forts were constructed at Columbia and
            Port Royal.

1719   November 28. The residents of South Caro-
            lina rebelled against the proprietary
            government and elected James Moore as
            governor. He served in the office until
            1721.

1721   May 29. Sir Francis Nicholson, the new
            royal governor, assumed his office. He
            served in this capacity until 1729.

1724   Arthur Middleton became president of the
            council and acting governor. He served in
            this capacity until 1729.

1792   July 25. South Carolina became a royal
            colony. King George II bought out seven
            of the eight proprietors.

            Robert Johnson became governor of the
            colony. He served in the post until
            1735.

1730   Estimated population: 30,000

            Governor Johnson arrived in South Caro-
            lina.

            The South Carolina Weekly Journal was
            published as the first newspaper in the
            colony. Only six issues were printed
            by 1737.

1735   Thomas Broughton became lieutenant gover-
            nor of the colony and served until 1737.

            The Friendly Society for the Mutual In-
            surance of Houses Against Fire was founded
            as probably the first fire insurance com-
            pany in the American colonies. The company
            was ruined as a result of the fire of No-
            vember 18, 1740 which destroyed half of
            Charleston.

1737   William Ball became president of the
            council and lieutenant-governor. He
            served in the posts until 1743.

1739   A group of slaves rebelled on the Storo
            River, stealing guns and killing 21 white
            colonists.

1740   Estimated population: 45,000.

            The slave code was revised as a result of
            the uprising in 1739.

1743   James Glen became governor of South Caro-
            lina and served in the office until 1756.

1750   Estimated population: 64,000.

1756   William Henry Lyttleton became governor
            of the colony and served in the post until
            1760.

1759   The Cherokee Indians rose up against the
            colonists.

1760   Estimated population: 94,074

            A war was fought against the Cherokee
            Indians, continuing until 1761.

            William Bull, the 2nd, became lieutenant
            governor of the colony and served until
            1761.

1761   Thomas Boone became governor and served
            in this capacity until 1764.

1764   William Bull, the 2nd, became lieutenant
            governor and served in the office until
            1766.

1765   August 2. South Carolina endorsed the

proposal of Massachusetts for a Stamp Act Congress. Thomas Lynch, Christopher Gadsden, and John Rutledge attended the Congress.

October 23. A mob in Charles Town searcged for stamps which they planned to confiscate.

1766 Lord Charles Greville Montague became governor of the colony. He served in the office until 1769.

1767 Spring. The Regulator campaign began. It was a spontaneous pursuit of various robber gangs by a number of neighborhood posses.

Andrew Jackson was born in Waxwau.

William Bull, the 2nd, again became lieutenant governor.

1768 January 29. Ocanee County was created, with Walhalla as its seat.

1769 July 22. South Carolina adopted an association.

William Bull, the 2nd, again served as lieutenant governor.

1770 Estimated population: 124,244.

June 28. The British fleet tried to capture Charleston. It was repulsed when it attacked Fort Moultrie.

The College of Charleston was founded. It received its charter in 1785 and was opened in 1790.

1771 The Exchange and Assembly Room opened in Charles Town.

Lord Charles Greville Montague became governor of South Carolina. He served in the office until 1773.

1773 December 22. Tea was landed in Charleston and stored in the government warehouse. It remained there until it was auctioned to raise funds in July 1776.

William Bull, the 2nd, again became lieutenant governor and served until 1775.

An intercommittee of correspondence was
appointed.

1775   June. The Council of Safety which had
been appointed by the Provincial Congress
virtually took charge of the government.
Henry Laurens became president of the
council and served until 1776.

September 15. Lord William Campbell, who
had become royal governor early in the year,
fled to a British warship.

1776   March 26. The first temporary constitution
was adopted.

June 4. The British moved against the palmetto log fort on Sullivan's Island, later
named Fort Moultrie for its defender.

John Rutledge became president of the state
in which position he served until 1778.

1778   March 19. The new constitution was adopted.

Henry Laurens, delegate from South Carolina,
presided over the Continental Congress.

Rawlins Lowndes became president of the state.
He served in the position until 1779.

1779   February 3. Moultrie was successful in
defending Port Royal.

February 14. Colonel Andrew Pickens defeated a Loyalist brigade at Kettle Creek.

John Rutledge became governor of the
state. He served in the post until 1782.

1780   Estimated population: 180,000.

May 12. General Benjamin Lincoln surrendered
Charleston to Sir Henry Clinton and his British troops in order to avoid destruction.
The British were then able to overrun the
state.

August 16. General Gates was defeated at
Camden by General Cornwallis.

October 7. American troops defeated the
British at King's Mountain in present-day
York County.

1781   April 19. General Greene was defeated by
the British at the Battle of Eutaw Springs.
General Greene withdrew on September 9.

1782   John Matthews became governor of South
Carolina and served in the office until
1783.

1783   Benjamin Guerard became governor of the
state. He served until 1785.

1785   March 12. The following counties were
created: Abbeville, Beaufort, Charleston,
Chester, Chesterfield, Clarendon, Colle-
ton, Darlington, Edgefield, Fairfield,
Greenville, Lancaster, Laurens, Lexington,
Marion, Marlboro, Newberry, Orangeburg,
Richland, Spartanburg, Union, Williamsburg,
and York.

Abbeville, with Abbeville as its seat, was
named for Abbeville, France. Beaufort,
with its seat at Beaufort, was named for
Beaufort, France and the Duke of Beaufort.
Charleston, with Charleston as its seat,
was named for King Charles II of England.

Chester, with Chester as its county seat,
was an adaptation of Cheshire, England.
Chesterfield, with its seat at Chesterfield,
was named for Philip Dormer Stanhope, fourth
earl of Chesterfield. Clarendon, with its
seat at Manning, was named for Edward Hyde
II, third earl of Clarendon, captain-general
and governor-in-chief of New York and
New Jersey.

Colleton, with Walterboro as its county seat,
was named for John Colleton, one of the
eight proprietors of South Carolina. Darlington, with its seat at Darlington, was
named for Darlington, England. Edgefield
has its seat at Edgefield. Fairfield has
Winnsboro as its county seat.

Greenville, with Greenville as its seat,
was either a descriptive term or was named
for Isaac Green who owned a mill in Reedy
River. The town grew around it. Lancaster,

with Lancaster as its seat, was named for
Lancaster, England.

Laurens, with its county seat at Laurens,
was named for Henry Laurens, president of
the Continental Congress, 1777-78, who was
named minister to Holland and was one of the
signers of the preliminary peace treaties
with Great Britain. Lexington, with its
seat at Lexington, was named for Lexington,
Massachusetts in commemoration of the battle
fought there early in the Revolutionary
War.

Marion, with Marion as its seat, was named
for Francis Marion, brigadier general in the
Revolutionary War who won the battle of
Eutaw Springs and later served in the South
Carolina Senate. Marlboro, with its county
seat at Bennettsville, was named for John
Churchill, duke of Marlborough, who won
victories at Blenheim, Ramilles and Mal-
plaquet.

Newberry has its seat at Newberry. Orangeburg, with Orangeburg as its seat, was
named for Prince William IV of Orange.
Richland has its seat at Columbia. Spartanburg has its county seat at Spartanburg.
Union has Union as its seat.

Williamsburg, with Kingstree as its seat,
was named for William III. York County,
with its seat at York, was named for James
II, formerly Duke of York.

William Moultrie became governor of South
Carolina. He served in the post until 1787.

1787   Thomas Pinckney became governor of the state.
        He served in this office until 1789.

1788   May 23. South Carolina ratified the United
        States Constitution, becoming the eighth
        state of the Union.

1789   January 26. Charles Pinckney, Democrat-
        Republican, became governor of South Caro-
        lina. He served in the office until De-
        cember 5, 1792.

1790   Population: 249,073.

January 19. The state legislature ratified the first Ten Amendments to the United States Constitution.

The new state constitution was adopted.

The College of Charleston was founded.

1791 Spring. President George Washington made a state visit to Charleston.

1792 December 5. William Moultrie, Federalist, became governor of the state. He served in the office until December 1794

1794 December. Arnoldus Vanderhorst, Democrat-Republican, became governor of Rhode Island in which post he served until 1796.

1796 Charles Pinckney, Democrat-Republican, became governor of the state. He served in the office until December 18, 1798.

1797 December 4. The state legislature ratified the 11th Amendment to the United States Constitution.

1798 December 18. Edward Rutledge, Democrat-Republican, became governor of South Carolina, serving in the office until his death on January 23, 1800.

1800 Population: 345,591.

January 23. John Drayton, Democrat-Republican, became governor of the state upon the death of Governor Rutledge. Drayton served in the post until December 1802.

1801 December 19. Harry County, with Conway as its seat, was established. It was named for Peter Harry who fought in the Revolutionary War.

The University of South Carolina was founded at Columbia.

1802 December. James B. Richardson, Democrat-Republican, became governor of the state in which position he served until December 1804.

1804   May 15. The state legislature ratified
            the 12th Amendment to the United States
            Constitution.

            December. Paul Hamilton, Democrat-Republi-
            can, became governor of the state. He
            served in the office until December 1806.

1805   December 14. The University of South Caro-
            lina which had originally been organized
            as South Carolina College became a state
            college. It granted its first degrees in
            1806.

1806   December. Charles Pinckney, Democrat-Re-
            publican, became governor of the state.
            He served in the office until December
            1808.

1808   December. John Drayton, Democrat-Republi-
            can, became governor of the state. He
            served in the gubernatorial office until
            December 1810.

1809   January 3. Darke County was created, with
            Greenville as its seat. It was named for
            William Darke, an Indian fighter and a
            delegate to the federal constitutional
            convention in 1788.

            March 7. Paul Hamilton was appointed Secre-
            tary of the Navy by President James Madison.
            Hamilton assumed his office as a member of
            the cabinet on May 15, 1809.

1810   Population: 415,115

            December. Henry Middleton, Democrat-Re-
            publican, became governor of the state.
            He served in the office until December 1812.

            December. Joseph Alston, Democrat-Repub-
            lican, became governor of South Carolina.
            He served in the office until December 1814.

1814   December. David R. Williams, Democrat-Re-
            publican, became governor of the state and
            served until December 1816.

1816   December. Andrew Pickens, Democrat-Repub-
            lican, became governor of South Carolina.
            He remained in the office until December
            1818.

1818   December. John Geddes, Democrat-Republi-
              can, became governor and served in the
              post until December 1820.

1820   Population: 502,741

              December. Thomas Bennett, Democrat-Repub-
              lican, became governor of the state. He
              served in this position until December
              1822.

1822   May 30. Denmark Vesey's slave conspiracy
              was discovered and suppressed in Charleston.
              Denmark Vesey was an emancipated Black who
              gathered a large group of Black city workers.

              December. John L. Wilson, Democrat-Republi-
              can, became governor of South Carolina.
              He served in the office until December 1824.

1824   December. Richard J. Manning, Democrat-
              Republican, became governor and remained
              in the office until December 1826.

1826   December. John Taylor, Democrat-Republican,
              became governor of the state. He served in
              this office until December 1828.

              December 20. Anderson and Pickens Counties
              were created. Anderson, with its seat at
              Anderson, was named for Robert Anderson,
              who served in the Revolutionary War.

              Pickens, with Pickens as its seat, was named
              for Andrew Pickens, who rose from captain
              to brigadier general during the Revolution-
              ary War and was also a United States Repre-
              sentative from South Carolina.

              Furman University was founded at Green-
              ville.

1828   December. Stephen D. Miller, Democrat, be-
              came governor of Rhode Island. He served in
              the office until December 1830.

              December 19. The South Carolina legislature
              adopted eight resolutions which declared
              the Tariff of Abominations was oppressive,
              unjust and unconstitutional.

1830   Population: 581,185

            December. James Hamilton, Jr., Democrat,
            became governor. He served in the office
            until December 1822.

1832   November 19. A state convention met at
            Columbia where it adopted an ordinance on
            November 24 which nullified the tariff laws
            of 1828 and 1832.

            November 27. The state legislature passed
            ;aws to enforce the nullification ordi-
            nance.

            December. Robert Y. Hayne, Democrat, be-
            came governor of South Carolina. He served
            in the office until December 11, 1834.

1833   March 15. The state convention met again
            and revoked the Ordinance of Nullification
            after the United States Congress had passed
            a law progressively reducing the tariff.

            March 18. The convention passed an ordinance
            to nullify the federal force act.

1834   December 11. George McDuffie, Democrat, be-
            came governor of the state and served in
            the office until December 1836.

1836   December. Pierce M. Butler, Democrat, be-
            came governor of South Carolina. He served
            until December 10, 1838.

1837   March 7. Joel R. Poinsett was appointed
            Secretary of War by President Martin Van
            Buren. Poinsett assumed his office as a
            member of the cabinet on March 14, 1837.

            The College of Charleston, which had opened
            in 1790, became the first municipal college
            in the nation.

1838   December 10. Patrick Noble, Democrat, be-
            came governor of South Carolina. He served
            in the office until his death on April 7,
            1840.

1839   Erskine College was founded at Due West.

1840   Population: 594,398.

April 7. Lieutenant Governor B. K. Henegan, Democrat, became acting governor of the state upon the death of Governor Patrick Noble. Henegan served in the office until the end of the term in December 1840.

December. Joel P. Richardson, Democrat, became governor of South Carolina. He served in the post until December 1842.

1841   September 13. Hugh S. Legaré was appointed Attorney General by President John Tyler. Legaré assumed his office as a member of the cabinet on September 20.

1842   December. James H. Hammond, Democrat, became governor of South Carolina. He served in the office until December 1844.

The Citadel was established in Charleston.

1844   March 6. John C. Calhoun was appointed Secretary of State by President John Tyler. Calhoun assumed his office as a member of the cabinet on April 1.

December. William Aiken, Democrat, became governor of South Carolina. He served in the post until December 1846

1845   Graniteville received its charter and actually represented one-half of the state's textile investment.

Limestone College was founded at Gaffney.

1846   December. David Johnson, Democrat, became governor of the state. He served in the office until December 1848.

1848   December. Whitemarsh B. Seabrook. Democrat, became governor. He served in the office until December 1850.

1850   Population: 668,507.

April. John C. Calhoun died a few months after his disunion speech was delivered for him in March.

1851   The Greenville district sent three unionists to the legislature.

1852   December. John C. Manning, Democrat, be-
                came governor of South Carolina. He served
                in the office until December 1854.

                Furman University was established at
                Greenville.

                William Gilmore Simms, Governor James H.
                Hammond and state Supreme Court chancellor
                William Harper published their views re-
                garding slavery in the Pro-Slavery Argu-
                ment.

1854   December. James H. Adams, Democrat, became
                governor of South Carolina. He served in
                the position until December 1856.

                Preston Brooks, United States Representative
                from South Carolina, attacked Senator Charles
                Sumner of Massachusetts with a cane, for
                having previously castigated Brooks' uncle,
                Senator Butler, in a speech in the Senate.
                Senator Sumner was incapacitated for several
                years. Brooks was censured. He resigned
                and was reelected to the House by a large
                majority.

                The following academic institutions were
                established: Columbia College at Columbia,
                Greenville Female College, and Wofford
                College at Spartanburg.

1856   December. Robert F. W. Allston, Democrat,
                became governor of South Carolina. He
                served in the office until December 1858.

                December 20. Newberry College received its
                charter at Newberry. Its first degrees were
                awarded in 1869. The college was moved to
                Walhalla in 1868 and then returned to New-
                berry in 1877.

1857   Paul Hamilton began publishing Russell's
                Magazine in Charleston.

1858   December. William H. Gist, Democrat, be-
                came governor. He served in the office un-
                til December 1860.

1859   The Due West Female College was organized
                at Due West.

1860   Population: 703,708.

April 23. The Democratic Party National
Convention convened in Charleston.

April 30. Southern delegates walked out
of the Democratic National Convention in
a dispute over the platform. The convention was adjourned on May 3 without naming
a presidential nominee.

December. Francis W. Pickens, Democrat,
became governor of South Carolina. He served
in the office until December 1862.

December 17. A state secession convention
met in the First Baptist Church at Columbia.

December 20. The secession convention
unanimously adopted the Ordinance of Secession at St. Andrew's Hall.

December 22. The state named three commissioners to arrange for the delivery of
public lands from the federal to the state
government.

December 27. The South Carolina troops
seized Fort Moultrie which had been
abandoned by Major Robert Anderson. Catle
Pinckney was also taken at this time.

December 30. State forces seized the federal
arsenal at Charleston.

1861   January 9. The South Carolina state battery fired on the unarmed United States supply ship, the Star of the West, in Charleston harbor. Governor Francis Wilkinson
Pickens gave the order to fire on the ship
which had been ordered to supply and rein-
force Fort Sumter by President James Buchan-
an.

February. Henry Timrod published his poem
"Ethnogenesis" which indicated a hope for
a Southern civilization. He later wrote
war poems and was given the title "laureate
of the Confederacy."

April 12. The Civil War began when General
Gustave Toutant Beauregard and his troops
fired on Fort Sumter in Charleston Harbor.
Major Anderson surrendered the fort when

his provisions ran out.

1862   December. Milledge L. Bonham, Democrat, became governor of South Carolina. He served in the office until December 1864.

1864   September. Confederate President Jefferson Davis paid a visit to Columbia.

December. Andrew G. McGrath, Democrat, became governor of the state. He served until June 1865.

1865   February 17. Confederate troops evacuated Columbia and set fire to the city, almost destroying it. General Sherman was threatening Columbia.

June. Benjamin F. Perry, Democrat, became provisional governor of the state. He served in this post until November 1865

November. After the new state constitution was adopted, James L. Orr, Conservative, became governor of the state. He was deposed by Act of Congress.

A Colored People's Convention met in Charleston where it protested the Blacks' menial status under the new state constitution.

November 13. The state legislature ratified the 13th Amendment to the United States Constitution.

1866   April 2. President Andrew Johnson declared that the insurrection was over in South Carolina.

Summer. The state legislature rejected the 14th Amendment to the United States Constitution.

1867   November. At the state elections 48 whites and 76 Blacks were elected to the state legislature.

1868   Spring. South Carolina adopted a new constitution.

June 25. South Carolina was readmitted to the Union when the United States Congress

passed an omnibus bill, granting the state
Congressional representation. This bill
was passed over President Johnson's veto.

July. Robert K. Scott became governor of
the state. He served in the office until
1872.

A free school system was created.

1869   March 15. The state legislature ratified
            the 15th Amendment to the United States
            Constitution.

            Claflin University for Blacks was founded
            at Orangeburg.

1870   Population: 705,606.

            Benedict College was established at
            Columbia.

1871   March 10. Aiken County, with its seat at
            Aiken, was created. It was named for Wil-
            liam Aiken, governor of South Carolina.

1872   Franklin J. Moses, Jr., Republican, became
            governor of South Carolina in which office
            he served until 1874.

            Lander Female College was founded at Wil-
            liamston. It became Williamston College
            in 1903.

1874   Daniel H. Chamberlain, Republican, became
            governor of the state. He served in the
            office until 1876.

1876   Wade Hampton, Democrat, became governor of
            South Carolina. He served in the office
            until his resignation in February 1879.

1877   March. Federal occupation of South Caro-
            lina ended.

            April 10. Carpet bag government ended when
            federal soldiers left Columbia.

1878   Hampton County, with its seat at Hampton,
            was founded. It was named for Wade Hampton,
            governor of the state.

1879   February. William D. Simpson, Democrat, became acting governor of South Carolina upon
the resignation of Governor Wade Hampton.
Simpson served in the office until his resignation in September 1880.

1880   Population: 995,577

September. Thomas D. Jeter, Democrat,
president of the state senate, became acting
governor upon the resignation of acting
governor William D. Simpson. Jeter served
in the post until the end of the term in
December.

December. Johnson Hagood, Democrat, became governor of South Carolina. He served
in the office until December 1882.

Presbyterian College was founded at Clinton.

1881   Allen University was created for Blacks
at Columbia.

1882   January 31. Berkeley County, with its
seat at Monck's Corner, was established.
It was named for Sir William Berkeley, governor of Virginia, who had put down Bacon's
Rebellion, and Sir William's brother,
John Berkeley, one of the eight original
proprietors.

December. Hugh S. Thompson, Democrat, became governor of the state. He served in
the office until his resignation in July
1886.

1886   July. Lieutenant Governor John C. Sheppard, Democrat, became acting governor of
the state upon the resignation of Governor
Hugh S. Thompson. Sheppard served until
the end of the term in December 1886.

December. John P. Richardson, Democrat
became governor of South Carolina in which
office he served until December 1890.

Winthrop College was founded at Rock Hill.

1888   December 22. Florence County, with its
seat at Florence, was created. It was
named for Florence Hardlee, daughter of

General W. W. Hardlee.

1889   Clemson Agricultural College, later Clemson University, and Converse College for women at Spartanburg were founded. Converse College was opened in 1890.

1890   Population: 1,151,149

The College for Women was established at Columbia.

December. Benjamin Ryan Tillman, Democrat, became governor of South Carolina. He served in the post until December 1894.

1892   Tillman's Dispensary Act, named for Governor Tillman, closed all barrooms, turning liquor sales over to public boards. It created the first state liquor monopoly in the nation. The residents of the state had indicated a desire for prohibition and were angry with Tillman for not pressing the issue completely.

1894   December. John Gary Evans, Democrat, became governor of South Carolina. He served in the office until January 1897.

1895   The state adopted its present constitution.

Winthrop Normal and Industrial College for Girls was founded at Rock Hill.

1896   February 25. Saluda County was established, with its seat at Saluda.

The Colored Normal, Industrial, Agricultural and Mechanical College was created.

South Carolina State College was founded at Orangeburg.

1897   January. William H. Ellerbe, Democrat, who had been elected in 1896, became governor of the state. He served in the office until his death on June 2, 1899.

February 25. Bamberg, Cherokee and Dorchester Counties were created. Bamberg, with its seat at Bamberg, was named for the Bamberg family. Cherokee, with Gaffney as its seat, was named for the Cherokee

Indians. Dorchester, with its county seat at St. George, was named for Dorchester, Massachusetts.

March 2. Greenwood County was established, with its seat at Greenwood.

Voorhees College was founded at Denmark.

1899   June 2. Lieutenant Governor Miles B. McSweeney, Democrat, became governor of South Carolina upon the death of Governor William H. Ellerbe. McSweeney served in the post until January 20, 1903.

1900   Population: 1,340,316.

1902   February 25. Lee County, with its seat at Bishopville, was established. It was named for Robert Edward Lee, a graduate of the United States Military Academy at West Point who served in the Mexican War. He joined the Confederate Army, becoming commander-in-chief of the southern forces in 1865. He later became president of Washington College.

1903   January 20. Duncan C. Heyward, Democrat, who had been elected in 1902, became governor of South Carolina. He served in the post until January 15, 1907.

1907   January 15. Martin F. Ansel, Democrat, who had been elected in 1906, became governor of the state. He served in this post until January 17, 1911.

1908   February 14. Calhoun County, with St. Matthews as its seat, was created. It was named for John Caldwell Calhoun, United States Representative and Senator from South Carolina, Vice President of the United States under Presidents John Quincy Adams and Andrew Jackson, and United States Secretary of State in the administration of President John Tyler.

Coker College was founded at Hartsville.

1910   Population: 1,515,400.

February 5. Dillon County, with Dillon as its seat, was established. It was named for J. W. Dillon.

February 19. The state legislature ratified the 16th Amendment to the United States Constitution.

1911 January 11. Coleman C. Blease, Democrat, became governor of the state. He had been elected in 1910 and served in the office until his resignation on January 14, 1915.

1912 January 30. Jasper County, with Carthage as its seat, was established. It was named for William Jasper who fought in the Revolutionary War and was killed in 1779 in the attack on Savannah.

1915 January 14. Lieutenant Governor Charles A. Smith, Democrat, became acting governor of the state upon the resignation of Governor Coleman L. Blease. Smith served several days until the end of the term on January 19, 1915.

January 19. Richard I. Manning, Democrat, who had been elected in 1914, became governor of South Carolina. He served in the of fice until January 21, 1919.

1916 February 19. McCormick County was created, with McCormick as its seat. It was named for Cyrus Hall McCormick, inventor of a successful reaper.

February 29. The state legislature passed child labor legislation which raised the minimum age for children to be employed in mills, factories and mines from the age of 12 to 14.

1918 January 29. The state legislature ratified the 18th Amendment to the United States Constitution.

1919 January 21. Robert A. Cooper, Democrat, who had been elected in 1918, became governor of the state. He served in the office until his resignation on May 20, 1922.

February 6. Allendale County, with its seat at Allendale, was created. It was named for Paul H. Allen, postmaster of

Allendale.

1920   Population: 1,683,724.

1922   May 20. Lieutenant Governor Wilson G.
            Harvey, Democrat, became governor of the
            state upon the resignation of Governor
            Robert A. Cooper. Harvey served in the
            office until January 16, 1923.

1923   January 16. Thomas G. McLeod, Democrat,
            who had been elected in 1922, became gover-
            nor of South Carolina. He served in the
            office until January 18, 1927.

1927   January 18. John G. Richards, Democrat,
            who had been elected in 1926, became gover-
            nor of the state. He served in the office
            until January 20, 1931.

1930   Population: 1,738,765.

            The first radio station began broadcasting
            at Spartanburg, WSPA.

1931   January 20. Ibra C. Blackwood, Democrat,
            who had been elected in 1930, became governor
            of the state. He served in the office
            until January 15, 1935.

1932   March 25. The state legislature ratified
            the 20th Amendment to the United States
            Constitution.

1933   March 4. Daniel C. Roper became Secretary
            of Commerce in the Cabinet of President
            Franklin D. Roosevelt.

1935   January 15. Olin D. Johnston, who had
            been elected in 1934, became governor of
            South Carolina. He served in the post
            until January 17, 1939.

1939   January 17. Burret R. Maybank, Democrat,
            who had been elected in 1938, became
            governor of the state. He served in the
            office until his resignation on November
            14, 1941.

1940   Population: 1, 899,804.

1941   November 4. Lieutenant Governor Joseph

E. Harley, Democrat, became governor of
the state upon the resignation of Governor Burnet R. Maybank. Harley served in
the office until his death on February
27, 1942.

The Santee Dam was finished. It began
supplying hydroelectric power for the
Charleston area.

1942   March 2. R. M. Jeffries, President of the
Senate, a Democrat, became governor of
the state upon the death of Governor Joseph
E. Harley. Jeffries served until the end
of the term on January 19, 1943.

1943   January 19. Olin D. Johnston, Democrat,
who had been elected in 1942, became governor of the state. He served in the post
until his resignation on January 2, 1945.

1945   January 2. Lieutenant Governor Ransome
J. Williams, Democrat, became governor of
South Carolina upon the resignation of
Governor Johnston. Williams was subse-
quently elected and served until January
21, 1947.

July 2. James F. Byrnes was appointed
Secretary of State by President Harry S.
Truman. Byrnes assumed his office as a
member of the cabinet on July 3, 1945.

1947   January 21. J. Strom Thurmond, Democrat,
who had been elected in 1946, became
governor of the state. He served in the
post until January 16, 1951.

1950   Population: 2,117,027.

1951   January 16. James F. Byrnes, Democrat,
who had been elected in 1950, became
governor of South Carolina. He served in
the office until January 18, 1955.

March 13. The state legislature ratified
the 22nd Amendment to the United States
Constitution.

1953   The state's first television station,
WCOS-TV, began broadcasting from
Columbia.

Operations began at the Atomic Energy Commission's Savannah River Plant near Aiken. The $1,400,000,000 plant would produce nuclear materials.

1954   May 17. The United States Supreme Court ruled in a case involving South Carolina that racial segregation in the public schools was unconstitutional.

November 13. Governor Byrnes signed a statement against school desegregation and in favor of maintaining state control of school policy. Governor-elect George Bell Timmerman also signed the statement.

1955   January 18. George Bell Timmerman, Jr., Democrat, who had been elected in 1954, became governor of South Carolina. He served in the office until January 20, 1959.

August 20. President Dwight D. Eisenhower declared South Carolina a major disaster area because of serious flooding.

1956   January 24. Governor George Bell Timmerman signed a four-state agreement with the governors of Georgia, Virginia, and Mississippi, whereby they agreed to cooperate in fighting the United States Supreme Court ruling against racial segregation in the public school systems.

1957   August 30. Senator Strom Thurman spoke for 24 hours and 27 minutes against civil rights, thus setting a new filibuster record.

1959   January 20. Ernest F. Hollings, Democrat, who had been elected in 1958, became governor of the state. He served in the post until January 15, 1963.

1960   Population: 2,382,594.

December 21. United States District Judge C. C. Wyche in Spartanburg rejected Harvey Gantt's suit to gain admission to the all-white state-owned Clemson College because Gantt did not comply with Clemson's application regulations. Gantt **failed** to prove discrimination.

1963   January 16. Donald S. Russell, Democrat,
            who had been elected in 1962, became gover-
            nor of the state. He served in the office
            until his resignation on April 22, 1965 to
            accept appointment as United States Senator
            from the state.

            January 28. Harvey B. Gantt, a Black stu-
            dent, enrolled in Clemson College, thus
            breaking segregation in the last state to
            hold out against integration.

            September. South Carolina schools continued
            to have prayers in spite of a June 17 Supreme
            Court ruling to the contrary.

            The state government established a birth
            control program.

1964   November. The residents of the state voted
            for Barry M. Goldwater, the first Republi-
            can candidate for President to carry the
            state since Reconstruction. Senator Strom
            Thurmond had resigned from the Democratic
            Party and became a Republican.

            The Baptist College of Charleston was
            founded.

1965   April 22. Lieutenant Governor Robert E.
            McNair, Democrat, became governor of the
            state upon the resignation of Governor
            Donald S. Russell. McNair was subsequently
            elected and served in the office until
            January 19, 1971.

1966   February 28. A three-judge federal court
            approved one of two plans submitted to re-
            apportion the state senate. The bill pro-
            viding for reapportionment had been signed
            by Governor Robert E. McNair on February
            3.

            November 8. State residents voted approval
            of an amendment to the state constitution
            permitting women to serve on juries.

1970   Population: 2,590,516.

            November. Three Black men were elected to
            the state legislature. They were the first
            Blacks to be elected to the General Assemb-
            ly since 1900.

Francis Marion College was founded at
Florence.

1971   January 19. John C. West, Democrat, who
            had been elected in 1970, became governor
            of South Carolina. He served in the gu-
            bernatorial office until January 21,
            1975.

            April 28. The state legislature ratified
            the 26th Amendment to the United States
            Constitution.

            The Medical University of South Carolina
            was founded at Charleston.

1972   December 6. Frederick P. Dent was appointed
            Secretary of Commerce by President Richard
            M. Nixon. Dent assumed his office as a
            member of the cabinet on January 18, 1973.

1974   November. James B. Edwards was elected the
            first Republican governor of the state
            since 1874.

1975   January 21. James Edwards, Republican,
            who had been elected in 1974, became
            governor of South Carolina.

            The state legislature rejected the Equal
            Rights Amendment to the United States
            Constitution.

1976   September 6. Democratic Presidential nomi-
            nee Jimmy Carter visited Darlington.

            October 23. President Gerald Ford visited
            Columbia as part of his campaign for the
            Presidency. He attended the Notre Dame-
            South Carolina football game.

1977   June 8. Governor James B. Edwards signed
            a bill which restored the state's death
            penalty.

BIOGRAPHICAL DIRECTORY

The selected list of governors, United States Senators and Members of the House of Representatives for South Carolina, 1789-1977, includes all persons listed in the Chronology for whom basic biographical data was readily available. Older biographical sources are frequently in conflict on certain individuals, and in such cases the source most commonly cited by later authorities was preferred.

ADAMS, James Hopkins
    Democrat
    b. South Carolina, March 15, 1812
    d. Columbia, S. C., July 13, 1861
    Governor of South Carolina, 1854-56

AIKEN, David Wyatt
    Democrat
    b. Winnsboro, S. C., March 17, 1828
    d. Cokesbury, S. C., April 6, 1887
    U. S. Representative, 1877-87

AIKEN, William
    Democrat
    b. Charleston, S. C., August 4, 1806
    d. Flat Rock, N. C., September 7, 1887
    Governor of South Carolina, 1844-46
    U. S. Representative, 1851-57

AIKEN, Wyatt
    Democrat
    b. near Macon, Ga., December 14, 1863
    d. Abbeville, S. C., February 6, 1923
    U. S. Representative, 1903-17

ALSTON, Joseph
    Democrat-Republican
    b. All Saints Parish, S. C., 1779
    d. September 10, 1816
    Governor of South Carolina, 1812-14

ALSTON, Lemuel Jones
    ----
    b. in the eastern part of Granville (now
        Warren) County, N. C., 1760
    d. "Alston Place," Clarke County, Ala., 1836
    U. S. Representative, 1807-11

ALSTON, Robert F. W.
    Governor of South Carolina, 1856-58

ANSEL, Martin Frederick
    b. Charleston, S. C., December 12, 1850
    d. ----
    Governor of South Carolina, 1907-11

ASHMORE, John Durant
    Democrat

    b. Greenville District, S. C., August 18, 1819
    d. Sardis, Miss., December 5, 1871
    U. S. Representative, 1859-60

ASHMORE, Robert Thomas
    Democrat
    b. on a farm near Greenville, S. C., Febru-
        ary 22, 1904
    U. S. Representative, 1953-69

BARNWELL, Robert
    Federalist
    d. Beaufort, S. C., December 21, 1761
    d. Beaufort, S. C., October 24, 1814
    Member Continental Congress, 1788-89
    U. S. Representative, 1791-93

BARNWELL, Robert Woodward
    Democrat
    b. Beaufort, S. C., August 10, 1801
    d. Columbia, S. C., November 24, 1882
    U. S. Representative, 1829-33
    U. S. Senator, 1850

BELLINGER, Joseph
    ----
    b. Bellinger Plantation in Saint Bartholomew
        Parish, Ashepoo, S. C., 1773
    d. Charleston, S. C., January 10, 1830
    U. S. Representative, 1817-19

BENET, Christie
    Democrat
    b. Abbeville, S. C., December 29, 1879
    d. Columbia, S. C., March 30, 1951
    U. S. Senator, 1918

BENNETT, Thomas
    Democrat-Republican
    Governor of South Carolina, 1820-22

BENTON, Lemuel
    Democrat
    b. Granville County, N. C., 1754
    d. Darlington, S. C., May 18, 1818
    U. S. Representative, 1793-99

BLACK, James Augustus
    Calhoun Democrat
    b. on his father's plantation in Ninety-
        Six District, near Abbeville, S. C., 1793
    d. Washington, D. C., April 3, 1848
    U. S. Representative, 1843-48

BLACKWOOD, Ibra C.
    Democrat
    Governor of South Carolina, 1931-35

BLAIR, James
    Democrat
    b. Waxhaw Settlement, Lancaster County,
        S. C., 1790
    d. Washington, D. C., April 1, 1834
    U. S. Representative, 1821-22 (Democrat),
        1829-31 (Union Democrat), 1831-34
        (Democrat)

BLEASE, Coleman Livingston
    Democrat
    b. near Newberry, S. C., October 8, 1868
    d. Columbia, S. C., January 19, 1942
    Governor of South Carolina, 1911-15
    U. S. Senator, 1925-31

BONHAM, Milledge Luke
    State Rights Democrat
    b. near Red Bank (now Saluda), Edgefield
        District, S. C., December 25, 1813
    d. White Sulphur Springs, N. C., April 27, 1890
    U. S. Representative, 1857-60
    Governor of South Carolina, 1862-64

BOWEN, Christopher Columbus
    Republican
    b. Providence, R. I., January 5, 1832
    d. New York, N. Y., June 23, 1880
    U. S. Representative, 1868-71

BOYCE, William Waters
    State Rights Democrat
    b. Charleston, S. C., October 24, 1818
    d. at his country home "Ashland," Fairfax
        County, Va., February 3, 1890
    U. S. Representative, 1853-60

BRATTON, John
    Democrat
    b. Winnsboro, S. C., March 7, 1831
    d. Winnsboro, S. C., January 12, 1898
    U. S. Representative, 1884-85

BRAWLEY, William Huggins
    Democrat
    b. Chester, S. C., May 13, 1841
    d. Charleston, S. C., November 15, 1916
    U. S. Representative, 1891-94

BREVARD, Joseph
    Whig
    b. Iredell, N. C., July 19, 1766
    d. Camden, S. C., October 11, 1821
    U. S. Representative, 1819-21

BROOKS, Preston Smith
    State Rights Democrat
    b. Edgefield District, S. C., August 5, 1819
    d. Washington, D. C., January 17, 1857
    U. S. Representative, 1853-56, 1856-57

BRYSON, Joseph Raleigh
    Democrat
    b. Brevard, N. C., January 18, 1893
    d. at the naval hospital, Bethesda, Md.,
        March 10, 1953
    U. S. Representative, 1939-53

BURKE, Aedanus
    ----
    b. Galway, Ireland, June 16, 1743
    d. Charleston, S. C., March 30, 1802
    U. S. Representative, 1789-91

BURT, Armistead
    Democrat
    b. Clouds Creek, near Edgefield, Edgefield
        District, S. C., November 13, 1802
    d. Abbeville, S. C., October 30, 1883
    U. S. Representative, 1843-53

BUTLER, Andrew Pickens
    State Rights Democrat
    b. Edgefield District, S. C., November 19, 1796
    d. near Edgefield, S. C., May 25, 1857
    U. S. Senator, 1846-57

BUTLER, Matthew Calbraith
    Democrat
    b. near Greenville, S. C., March 8, 1836
    d. Columbia, S. C., April 14, 1909
    U. S. Senator, 1877-95

BUTLER, Pierce
    Democrat
    b. Ireland, July 11, 1744
    d. Philadelphia, Pa., February 15, 1822
    Member Continental Congress, 1787-88
    U. S. Senator, 1789-96, 1802-04

BUTLER, Pierce Mason

Democrat
b. Mt. Willing, S. C., April 11, 1798
d. at Battle of Chuburusco, Mexico, August 20, 1847
Governor of South Carolina, 1836-38

BUTLER, Sampson Hale
Democrat
b. near Ninety-Six, Edgefield District,
    S.C., January 3, 1803
d. Tallahassee, Fla., March 16, 1848
U. S. Representative, 1839-42

BUTLER, William
Anti-Federalist
b. Prince William County, Va., December 17, 1759
d. on his plantation on the Saluda River
    near Mount Willing, S. C., September 15, 1821
U. S. Representative, 1801-13

BUTLER, William (son of the preceding)
Whig
b. Edgefield District, S. C., February 1, 1790
d. Fort Gibson, Indian Territory (now Okla-
    homa), September 25, 1850
U. S. Representative, 1841-43

BUTTZ, Charles Wilson   **2031555**
Republican
b. Stroudsburg, Pa., November 16, 1837
d. Lisbon, N. D., July 20, 1913
U. S. Representative, 1876-77

BYRNES, James Francis
Democrat
b. Charleston, S. C., May 2, 1879
U. S. Representative, 1911-25
U. S. Senator, 1931-41
Associate Justice of the U. S. Supreme
    Court, 1941-42
U. S. Secretary of State, 1945-47
Governor of South Carolina, 1951-55

CAIN, Richard Harvey
Republican
b. Greenbrier County, Va., April 12, 1825
d. Washington, D. C., January 18, 1887
U. S. Representative, 1873-75, 1877-79

CALDWELL, Patrick Calhoun
State Rights Democrat
b. Newberry, S. C., March 10, 1801
d. South Carolina, November 22m 1855
U. S. Representative, 1841-43

36   SOUTH CAROLINA

CALHOUN, John Caldwell
    War Democrat
    b. Calhoun Mills, Abbeville District, S. C.,
        March 18, 1782
    d. Washington, D. C., March 31, 1850
    U. S. Representative, 1811-17
    U. S. Secretary of War, 1817-25
    Vice President of the United States, 1825-32
    U. S. Senator, 1832-43
    U. S. Secretary of State, 1844-45
    U. S. Senator, 1845-50

CALHOUN, Joseph
    Democrat
    b. Staunton, Va., October 22, 1750
    d. Calhoun Mills, Abbeville District, S. C.,
        April 14, 1817
    U. S. Representative, 1807-11

CAMPBELL, John
    State Rights Democrat
    b. Brownsville, S. C.
    d. Parnassus, S. C., May 19, 1845
    U. S. Representative, 1829-31 (**State Rights
        Whig**), 1837-45 (State Rights Democrat)

CAMPBELL, Robert Blair
    Whig
    b. Marlboro County, S. C.
    d. Ealing, London, England, July 12, 1862
    U. S. Representative, 1823-25 (----), 1834-
        35 (Nullificationist), 1835-37 (Whig)

CARPENTER, Lewis Cass
    Republican
    b. Putnam, Conn., February 20, 1836
    d. Denver, Colo., March 6, 1908
    U. S. Representative, 1874-75

CARTER, John
    ----
    b. Camden, Sumter District, S. C., September
        10, 1792
    d. Georgetown, D. C., June 20, 1850
    U.S. Representative, 1822-29

CASEY, Levi
    ----
    b. South Carolina, approximately 1752
    d. Washington, D. C., February 3, 1807
    U. S. Representative, 1803-07

CHAMBERLAIN, Daniel Henry

Republican
b. W. Brookfield, Mass., June 23, 1835
d. 1907
Governor of South Carolina, 1874-76

CHAPPELL, John Joel
State Rights War Democrat
b. Columbia, S. C., January 19, 1782
d. Lowndes County, Ala., May 23, 1871
U. S. Representative, 1813-17

CHESTNUT, James, Jr.
State Rights Democrat
b. Camden, S. C., January 18, 1815
d. Camden, S. C., February 1, 1885
U. S. Senator, 1858-60

CHEVES, Langdon
Democrat
b. Bulltown Fort, near Rocky River, Ninety
    Six District, S. C., September 17, 1776
d. Columbia, S. C., June 26, 1857
U. S. Representative, 1810-15; Speaker, 1814-15

CLOWNEY, William
State Rights Democrat
b. Union County, S. C., March 21, 1797
d. Union, S. C., March 12, 1851
U. S. Representative, 1833-35 (Nullifier),
    1837-39 (State Rights Democrat)

COLCOCK, William Ferguson
Democrat
b. Beaufort, S. C., November 5, 1804
d. McPhersonville, S. C., June 13, 1889
U. S. Representative, 1849-53

COLHOUN, John Ewing
Democrat
b. Staunton, Va., 1750
d. Pendleton, S. C., October 26, 1802
U. S. Senator, 1801-02

COOPER, Robert Archer
Democrat
b. Laurens County, S. C., June 12, 1874
d. August 7, 1953
Governor of South Carolina, 1919-22
U. S. District Judge, District of Puerto
    Rico, 1934-47

CORLEY, Manuel Simeon
Republican

b. Lexington County, S. C., February 10, 1823
d. Lexington, S. C., November 20, 1902
U. S. Representative, 1868-69

COTRAN, James Sproull
Democrat
b. Abbeville, S. C., August 8, 1830
d. New York, N. Y., December 5, 1897
U. S. Representative, 1887-91

CROFT, George William
Democrat
b. Newberry County, S. C., December 20, 1846
d. Aiken, S. C., March 10, 1904
U. S. Representative, 1903-04

CROFT, Theodore Gaillard
Democrat
b. Aiken, S. C., November 26, 1874
d. Aiken, S. C., March 23, 1920
U. S. Representative, 1904-05

DANIEL, Charles Ezra
Democrat
b. Elberton, Ga., November 11, 1895
d. Greenville, S. C., September 13, 1964
U. S. Senator, 1954

DARGAN, George William
Democrat
b. Darlington, S. C., May 11, 1841
d. Darlington, S. C., June 29, 1898
U. S. Representative, 1883-91

DAVIS, Mendel J.
Democrat
b. October 23, 1942
U. S. Representative, 1971-

DAVIS, Warren Ransom
State Rights Democrat
b. Columbia, S. C., May 8, 1793
d. Washington, D. C., January 29, 1835
U. S. Representative, 1827-35

DE LARGE, Robert Carlos
Republican
b. Aiken, S. C., March 15, 1842
d. Charleston, S. C., February 14, 1874
U. S. Representative, 1871-73

DENHOLM, Frank E.
Democrat
b. November 29, 1923

U. S. Representative, 1971-

DE SAUSSURE, William Ford
    Democrat
    b. Charleston, S. C., February 22, 1792
    d. Columbia, S. C., March 13, 1870
    U. S. Senator, 1852-53

DIAL, Nathaniel Barksdale
    Democrat
    b. near Laurens, S. C., April 24, 1862
    d. Washington, D. C., December 11, 1940
    U. S. Senator, 1919-25

DIBBLE, Samuel
    Democrat
    b. Charleston, S. C., September 16, 1837
    d. near Baltimore, Md., September 16, 1913
    U. S. Representative, 1881-82, 1883-91

DORN, William Jennings Bryan
    Democrat
    b. near Greenwood, S. C., April 14, 1916
    U. S. Representative, 1947-49, 1951-

DRAYTON, John
    Democrat-Republican
    b. Charleston, S. C., June 22, 1767
    d. Charleston, S. C., November 27, 1822
    Governor of South Carolina, 1800-02, 1808-10

DRAYTON, William
    Union Democrat
    b. St. Augustine, Fla., December 30, 1776
    d. Philadelphia, Pa., May 24, 1846
    U. S. Representative, 1825-33

EARLE, Elias
    Democrat
    b. Frederick County, Va., June 19, 1792
    d. Centerville, S. C., May 19, 1823
    U. S. Representative, 1805-07, 1811-15, 1817-21

EARLE, John Baylis
    ----
    b. on the North Carolina side of the North
        Pacolet River, near Landrum, S. C.,
        October 23, 1766
    d. Anderson County, S. C., February 3, 1863
    U. S. Representative, 1803-05

EARLE, Joseph Haynsworth
    Democrat

b. Greenville, S. C., April 30, 1847
d. Greenville, S. C., May 20, 1897
U. S. Senator, 1897

EARLE, Samuel
- - - -
b. Frederick County, Va., November 28, 1760
d. Pendleton District, S. C., November 24, 1833
U. S. Representative, 1795-97

EDWARDS, James Burrows
Republican
b. Hawthorne, Fla., June 24, 1927
Governor of South Carolina, 1975-

ELLERBE, James Edwin
Democrat
b. Sellers, S. C., January 12, 1867
d. Asheville, S. C., October 24, 1917
U. S. Representative, 1905-13

ELLERBE, William Haselden
Democrat
b. Marion County, S. C., April 7, 1862
d. 1899
Governor of South Carolina, 1897-99

ELLIOTT, Robert Brown
Republican
b. Boston, Mass., August 11, 1842
d. New Orleans, La., August 9, 1884
U. S. Representative, 1871-74

ELLIOTT, William
Democrat
b. Beaufort, S. C., September 3, 1838
d. Beaufort, S. C., December 7, 1907
U. S. Representative, 1887-90, 1891-93,
    1895-96, 1897-1903

ELMORE, Franklin Harper
State Rights Democrat
b. Laurens District, S. C., October 15, 1799
d. Washington, D. C., May 28, 1850
U. S. Representative, 1836-39
U. S. Senator, 1850

ERVIN, James
Protectionist
b. Williamsburg District, S. C., October 17, 1778
d. Darlington, S. C., July 7, 1841
U. S. Representative, 1817-21

EVANS, David Reid
Democrat
b. Westminster, England, February 20, 1769
d. Winnsboro, S. C., March 8, 1843
U. S. Representative, 1813-15

EVANS, John Gary
Democrat
b. Cokesbury, S. C., October 15, 1863
d. June 27, 1942
Governor of South Carolina, 1894-97

EVANS, Josiah James
State Rights Democrat
b. Marlboro District, S. C., November 27, 1786
d. Washington, D. C., May 6, 1858
U. S. Senator, 1853-58

EVINS, John Hamilton
Democrat
b. Spartanburg District, S. C., July 18, 1830
d. Spartanburg, S. C., October 20, 1884
U. S. Representative, 1877-84

FARROW, Samuel
War Democrat
b. Virginia, 1759
d. Columbia, S. C., November 18, 1824
U. S. Representative, 1813-15

FELDER, John Meyers
Democrat
b. Orangeburg District, S. C., July 7, 1782
d. Union Point, Ga., September 1, 1851
U. S. Representative, 1831-35

FINLEY, David Edward
Democrat
b. Trenton, Ark., February 28, 1861
d. Charlotte, N. C., January 26, 1917
U. S. Representative, 1899-1917

FULMER, Hampton Pitts
Democrat
b. near Springfield, S. C., June 23, 1875
d. Washington, D. C., October 19, 1944
U. S. Representative, 1921-44

FULMER, Willa Lybrand
Democrat
b. Wagener, S. C., February 3, 1884
d. on board a ship en route to Europe,
   May 13, 1968

U. S. Representative, 1944-45

GAILLARD, John
Democrat
b. St. Stephens District, S. C., September 5, 1765
d. Washington, D. C., February 26, 1826
U.S. Senator, 1804-26; President pro tempore,
1809-10, 1814-18, 1819-25

GARY, Frank Boyd
Democrat
b. Cokesbury, S. C., March 9, 1860
d. Charleston, S. C., December 7, 1922
U. S. Senator, 1908-09

GASQUE, Allard Henry
Democrat
b. on Friendfield plantation, near Hyman,
S. C., March 8, 1873
d. Washington, D. C., June 17, 1938
U. S. Representative, 1923-38

GASQUE, Elizabeth Hawley
Democrat
b. near Blythewood, on Rice Plantation,
S. C.
U. S. Representative, 1938-39

GEDDES, John
Democrat-Republican
Governor of South Carolina, 1818-20

GETTYS, Thomas Smithwock
Democrat
b. Rockhill, S. C., June 19, 1912
U. S. Representative, 1964-

GILLON, Alexander
----
b. Rotterdam, Holland, 1741
d. on his plantation "Gillon's Retreat,"
Orangeburg District, S. C., October 6, 1794
U. S. Representative, 1793-94

GIST, Joseph
Democrat
b. near the mouth of Fair Forest Creek,
S. C., January 12,1775
d. Pinckneville, S. C., March 8, 1836
U. S. Representative, 1821-27

GIST, William Henry
Democrat

b. Charleston, S. C., August 22, 1807
d. Union District, S. C., September 30, 1874
Governor of South Carolina, 1858-60

GOSS, James Hamilton
Republican
b. Union, S. C., August 9, 1820
d. Union, S. C., October 31, 1886
U. S. Representative, 1868-69

GOURDIN, Theodore
Democrat
b. near Kingstree, S. C., March 20, 1764
d. Pineville, S. C., January 17, 1826
U. S. Representative, 1813-15

GOVAN, Andrew Robison
----
b. Orange Parish, S. C., January 13, 1794
d. Marshall County, Miss., June 27, 1841
U. S. Representative, 1822-27

GRAYSON, William John
Whig
b. Beaufort, S. C., November 2, 1788
d. Newberry, S. C., October 4, 1863
U. S. Representative, 1833-37

GRIFFIN, John King
State Rights Whig
b. near Clinton, S. C., August 13, 1789
d. near Clinton, S. C., August 1, 1841
U. S. Representative, 1831-41

HAGOOD, Johnson
Democrat
b. Barnwell County, S. C.
d. Barnwell, S. C., January 4, 1898
Governor of South Carolina, 1880-82

HALL, Wilton Earle
Democrat
b. Starr, Hall Township, S. C., March 11, 1901
U. S. Senator, 1944-45

HAMILTON, James, Jr.
State Rights Free Trader
b. Charleston, S. C., May 8, 1786
d. by drowning on the way from New Orleans
    to Galveston, Tex., November 15, 1857
U. S. Representative, 1822-29
Governor of South Carolina, 1830-32

HAMILTON, Paul
    Democrat-Republican
    b. St. Paul's Parish, S. C.
    d. Beaufort, S. C., June 30, 1816
    Governor of South Carolina, 1804-06
    U. S. Secretary of the Navy, 1809-13

HAMMOND, James Henry
    State Rights Democrat
    b. Newberry District, S. C., November 15, 1807
    d. "Redcliffe," Beach Island, S. C.,
        November 13, 1864
    U. S. Representative, 1835-36 (State Rights
        Free Trader)
    Governor of South Carolina, 1842-44
    U. S. Senator, 1857-60 (State Rights Democrat)

HAMPTON, Wade
    Democrat
    b. Virginia, 1752
    d. Columbia, S. C., February 4, 1835
    U. S. Representative, 1795-97, 1803-05

HAMPTON, Wade (grandson of the preceding)
    Democrat
    b. Charleston, S. C., March 28, 1818
    d. Columbia, S. C., April 11, 1902
    Governor of South Carolina, 1876-79
    U. S. Senator, 1879-91

HARE, Butler
    Democrat
    b. on a farm in Edgefield (now Saluda) County,
        near Leesville, S. C., November 25, 1875
    d. Saluda, S. C., December 30, 1967
    U. S. Representative, 1925-33, 1939-47

HARE, James Butler
    Democrat
    b. Saluda, S. C., September 4, 1918
    d. Columbia, S. C., July 16, 1966
    U. S. Representative, 1949-51

HARLEY, Joseph
    Democrat
    Governor of South Carolina, 1941-42

HARPER, Robert Goodloe
    Federalist (South Carolina/Maryland)
    b. near Fredericksburg, Va., January 1765
    d. Baltimore, Md., January 14, 1825
    U. S. Representative, 1795-1801 (South Carolina)
    U. S. Senator, 1816 (Maryland)

HARPER, William
    State Rights Democrat
    b. on the island of Antigua, West Indies,
        January 17, 1790
    d. Fairfield District, S. C., October 10, 1847
    U. S. Senator, 1826

HARVEY, Wilson G.
    Democrat
    Governor of South Carolina, 1922-23

HAYNE, Arthur Peronneau
    Democrat
    b. Charleston, S. C., March 12, 1790
    d. Charleston, S. C., January 7, 1867
    U. S. Senator, 1858

HAYNE, Robert Young
    Tariff Democrat
    b. on Pon Pon Plantation, St. Paul's Parish,
        Colleton District, S. C., November 10, 1791
    d. Asheville, N. C., September 24, 1839
    U. S. Senator, 1823-32
    Governor of South Carolina, 1832-34

HEMPHILL, John James
    Democrat
    b. Chester, S. C., August 25, 1849
    d. Washington, D. C., May 11, 1912
    U. S. Representative, 1883-93

HEMPHILL, Robert Witherspoon
    Democrat
    b. Chester, S. C., May 10, 1915
    U. S. Representative, 1957-64

HENAGAN, B. K.
    Democrat
    Governor of South Carolina, 1840

HEYWARD, Duncan C.
    Democrat
    Governor of South Carolina, 1903-07

HOGE, Solomon Lafayette
    Republican
    b. Pickreltown, Ohio, July 11, 1836
    d. Battle Creek, Mich., February 23, 1909
    U. S. Representative, 1869-71, 1875-77

HOLLINGS, Ernest F.
    Democrat
    b. Charleston, S. C., January 1, 1922

U. S. Representative, 1959-63
U. S. Senator, 1966-

HOLMES, Isaac Edward
    Democrat
    b. Charleston, S. C., April 6, 1796
    d. Charleston, S. C., February 24, 1867
    U. S. Representative, 1839-51

HORST, Arnoldus Vander
    Federalist
    Governor of South Carolina, 1794-96

HUNTER, John
    Federalist
    b. South Carolina, 1732
    d. on his plantation, S. C., 1802
    U. S. Representative, 1793-95
    U. S. Senator, 1796-98

IRBY, John Laurens Manning
    Democrat
    b. Laurens, S. C., September 10, 1854
    d. Laurens, S. C., December 9, 1900
    U. S. Senator, 1891-97

ISLAR, James Ferdinand
    Democrat
    b. near Orangeburg, S. C., November 25, 1832
    d. Orangeburg, S. C., May 26, 1912
    U. S. Representative, 1894-95

JEFFRIES, Richard M.
    Democrat
    Governor of South Carolina, 1942-43

JETER, Thomas B.
    Democrat
    Governor of South Carolina, 1880

JOHNSON, David
    Democrat
    Governor of South Carolina, 1846-48

JOHNSON, Joseph Travis
    Democrat
    b. Brewerton, S. C., February 28, 1858
    d. Spartanburg, S. C., May 8, 1919
    U. S. Representative, 1901-15

JOHNSTON, Olin Dewitt Talmadge
    Democrat
    b. near Honea Path, S. C., November 18, 1896

d. Columbia, S. C., April 18, 1965
Governor of South Carolina, 1935-39, 1943-45
U. S. Senator, 1945-65

JOHNSTONE, George
Democrat
b. Newberry, S. C., April 18, 1846
d. Newberry, S. C., March 8, 1921
U. S. Representative, 1891-93

KEITT, Laurence Massillon
Democrat
b. Orangeburg District, S. C., October 4, 1824
d. the day after he was wounded in the Battle
    of Cold Harbor, near Richmond, Va.,
    June 4, 1864
U. S. Representative, 1853-56, 1856-60

KERSHAM, John
Democrat
b. Camden, S. C., September 12, 1765
d. Camden, S. C., August 4, 1829
U. S. Representative, 1813-15

LATIMER, Asbury Churchwell
Democrat
b. near Lowndesville, S. C., July 31, 1851
d. Washington, D. C., February 20, 1908
U. S. Representative, 1893-1903
U. S. Senator, 1903-08

LEGARE, George Swinton
Democrat
b. Rockville, S. C., November 11, 1869
d. Charleston, S. C., January 31, 1913
U. S. Representative, 1903-13

LEGARE, Hugh Swinton
Union Democrat
b. Charleston, S. C., January 2, 1797
d. Boston, Mass., June 20, 1843
U. S. Representative, 1837-39
U. S. Attorney General, 1841-43
U. S. Secretary of State, 1843

LEVER, Asbury Francis
Democrat
b. near Springhill, S. C., January 5, 1875
d. at "Seven Oaks," near Charleston, S. C.,
    April 28, 1940
U. S. Representative, 1901-19

LOGAN, William Turner
Democrat

b. Summerville, S. C., June 21, 1874
d. Charleston, S. C., September 15, 1941
U. S. Representative, 1921-25

LOWNDES, Thomas
    Federalist
    b. Charleston, S. C., January 22, 1766
    d. Charleston, S. C., July 8, 1843
    U. S. Representative, 1801-05

LOWNDES, William
    Democrat
    b. on "Horseshoe" Plantation near Jackson-
       borough, St. Bartholomew's Parish, S. C.,
       February 11, 1782
    d. at sea en route to England, May 8, 1822
    U. S. Representative, 1811-22

LUMPKIN, Alva Moore
    Democrat
    b. Milledgeville, Ga., November 13, 1886
    d. Washington, D. C., August 1, 1941
    U. S. Senator, 1941

MACKEY, Edmund McGregor
    Republican
    b. Charleston, S. C., March 8, 1846
    d. Washington, D. C., January 27, 1884
    U. S. Representative, 1875-76 (Independent
      Republican), 1882-84 (Republican)

MAGRATH, Andrew Gordon
    Democrat
    b. Charleston, S. C., February 8, 1813
    d. Charleston, S. C., April 9, 1893
    Governor of South Carolina, 1864-65

MAHON, Gabriel Heyward, Jr.
    Democrat
    b. Williamston, S. C., November 11, 1889
    d. Greenville, S. C., June 11, 1962
    U. S. Representative, 1936-39

MANN, Edward Coke
    Democrat
    b. Lowndesville, S. C., November 21, 1880
    d. near Rowesville, S. C., November 11, 1931
    U. S. Representative, 1919-21

MANN, James Robert
    Democrat
    b. Greenville, S. C., April 27, 1920
    U. S. Representative, 1969-

MANNING, Richard Irvine
Democrat
b. near Sumter, S. C., May 1, 1789
d. Philadelphia, Pa., May 1, 1836
Governor of South Carolina, 1824-26
U. S. Representative, 1834-36

MARION, Robert
----
b. Berkeley District, S. C.
d. ----
U. S. Representative, 1805-10

MARTIN, William Dickinson
Democrat
b. Martintown, Edgefield District, S. C.,
October 20, 1789
d. Charleston, S. C., November 17, 1833
U. S. Representative, 1827-31

MAYBANK, Burnet Rhett
Democrat
b. Charleston, S. C., March 7, 1899
d. at his summer home, Flat Rock, September
1, 1954
Governor of South Carolina, 1939-41
U. S. Senator, 1941-54

MAYRANT, William
----
b. South Carolina
d. ----
U. S. Representative, 1815-16

MCCORKLE, Paul Grier
Democrat
b. Yorkville (now York), S. C., December
19, 1863
d. Knoxville, Tenn., June 2, 1934
U. S. Representative, 1917

MCCREARY, John
----
b. near Fishing Creek, about 18 miles from
Chester, S. C., 1761
d. on his plantation, S. C., November 4, 1833
U. S. Representative, 1819-21

MCDUFFIE, George
Democrat
b. Columbia County, Ga., August 10, 1790
d. Cherry Hill, S. C., March 11, 1851
U. S. Representative, 1821-34

Governor of South Carolina, 1834-36
U. S. Senator, 1842-46

MCLAURIN, John Lowndes
    Democrat
    b. Red Bluff, S. C., May 9, 1860
    d. at his estate near Bennettsville, S. C.,
        July 29, 1934
    U. S. Representative, 1892-97
    U. S. Senator, 1897-1903

MCLEOD, Thomas G.
    Democrat
    Governor of South Carolina, 1923-27

MCMILLAN, Clara Gooding
    Democrat
    b. Brunson, S. C., August 17, 1894
    U. S. Representative, 1939-41
    Liason officer, Department of State, 1946-57

MCMILLAN, John Lanneau
    Democrat
    b. on a farm near Mullins, S. C., April 22, 1898
    U. S. Representative, 1939-

MCMILLAN, Thomas Sanders
    Democrat
    b. near Ulmers, S. C., November 27, 1888
    d. Charleston, S. C., September 29, 1939
    U. S. Representative, 1925-39

MCNAIR, Robert Evander
    Democrat
    b. Cades, S. C., December 14, 1923
    Governor of South Carolina, 1965-71

MCQUEEN, John Democrat
    b. Queensdale, near the town of Maxton,
        February 9, 1804
    d. Society Hill, S. C., August 30, 1867
    U. S. Representative, 1849-60

MCSWAIN, John Jackson
    Democrat
    b. on a farm near Cross Hill, S. C., May 1, 1875
    d. Columbia, S. C., August 6, 1936
    U. S. Representative, 1921-36

MEANS, John Hugh
    Democrat
    Governor of South Carolina, 1850-52

MIDDLETON, Henry
Democrat
b. London, England, September 28, 1770
d. Charleston, S. C., June 14, 1846
Governor of South Carolina, 1811-12
U. S. Representative, 1815-19

MILES, William Porcher
Democrat
b. Charleston, S. C., July 4, 1822
d. Burnside, La., May 11, 1899
U. S. Representative, 1857-60

MILLER, Stephen Decatur
Nullifier
b. Waxhaw Settlement, Lancaster District,
   S. C., May 8, 1787
d. Raymond, Miss., March 8, 1838
U. S. Representative, 1817-19 (Democrat)
Governor of South Carolina, 1828-30
U. S. Senator, 1831-33 (Nullifier)

MILLER, Thomas Ezekiel
Republican
b. Ferrebeville, S. C., June 17, 1849
d. Charleston, S. C., April 8, 1938
U. S. Representative, 1890-91

MITCHELL, Thomas Rothmaler
----
b. Georgetown, S. C., May 1783
d. Georgetown, S. C., November 2, 1837
U. S. Representative, 1821-23, 1825-29, 1831-33

MOORE, Thomas
----
b. Spartanburg District, S. C., 1759
d. near Moore's Station, S. C., July 11, 1822
U. S. Representative, 1801-13, 1815-17

MOSES, Franklin J., Jr.
Republican
Governor of South Carolina, 1872-74

MOULTRIE, William
Federalist
b. Charlestown (now Charleston), S. C.,
   November 23, 1730
d. Charlestown, S. C., September 27, 1805
Governor of South Carolina, 1792-94

MURRAY, George Washington
Republican

b. near Rembert, S. C., September 22, 1853
d. Chicago, Ill., April 21, 1926
U. S. Representative, 1893-95, 1896-97

NESBITT, Wilson
    Democrat
    b. ----
    d. Montgomery, Ala., May 13, 1861
    U. S. Representative, 1813-19

NICHOLLS, Samuel Jones
    Democrat
    b. Spartanburg, S. C., May 7, 1885
    d. Spartanburg, S. C., November 23, 1937
    U. S. Representative, 1915-21

NOBLE, Patrick
    Democrat
    Governor of South Carolina, 1838-40

NORTON, James
    Democrat
    b. near Mullins, S. C., October 8, 1843
    d. Mullins, S. C., October 14, 1920
    U. S. Representative, 1897-1901

NOTT, Abraham
    Federalist
    b. Saybrook, Conn., February 5, 1768
    d. Fairfield, S. C., June 19, 1830
    U. S. Representative, 1799-1801

NUCKOLLS, William Thompson
    ----
    b. near Hancockville, S. C., February 23, 1801
    d. on his plantation near Hancockville,
        S. C., September 27, 1855
    U. S. Representative, 1827-33

O'CONNOR, Michael Patrick
    Democrat
    b. Beaufort, S. C., September 29, 1831
    d. Charleston, S. C., April 26, 1881
    U. S. Representative, 1879-81

ORR, James Lawrence
    Democrat
    b. Craytonville, S. C., May 12, 1822
    d. St. Petersburg, Russia, May 5, 1873
    U. S. Representative, 1849-59; Speaker, 1857-59
    Governor of South Carolina, 1867 (Republican)
    U. S. Minister to Russia, 1872-73

OVERSTREET, James
----
b. near Barnwell Court House, S. C., February 11, 1773
d. en route to his home from Washington, D. C., May 24, 1822
U. S. Representative, 1819-22

PATTERSON, James O'Hanlon
Democrat
b. Barnwell, S. C., June 25, 1857
d. Barnwell, S. C., October 25, 1911
U. S. Representative, 1905-11

PATTERSON, John James
Republican
b. Waterloo, Pa., August 8, 1830
d. Mifflinton, Pa., September 28, 1912
U. S. Senator, 1873-79

PEACE, Roger Craft
Democrat
b. Greenville, S. C., May 19, 1894
d. Greenville, S. C., August 20, 1968
U. S. Senator, 1941

PERRY, Benjamin Franklin
b. Pendleton District, S. C., November 20, 1805
d. Greenville, S. C., December 3, 1886
Governor of South Carolina, 1865

PERRY, William Hayne
Democrat
b. Greenville, S. C., June 9, 1839
d. at his home "Sans Souci," near Greenville, S. C., July 7, 1902
U. S. Representative, 1885-91

PICKENS, Andrew
Democrat
b. Paxton, Pa., September 13, 1739
d. Tomassee, S. C., August 11, 1817
U. S. Representative, 1793-95

PICKENS, Francis Wilkinson
Nullifier Democrat
b. on a plantation on the Toogoodoo River, St. Pauls Parish, Colleton District, S. C., April 7, 1805
d. Edgefield, S. C., January 25, 1869
U. S. Representative, 1834-43
Governor of South Carolina, 1860-62

PINCKNEY, Charles
    Democrat
    b. Charles Town (now Charleston), S. C.,
        October 26, 1757
    d. Charleston, S. C., October 29, 1824
    Member Continental Congress, 1777-78, 1784-87
    Governor of South Carolina, 1789-92, 1796-98
    U. S. Senator, 1798-1801
    Governor of South Carolina, 1806-08
    U. S. Representative, 1819-21

PINCKNEY, Henry Laurens
    Democrat
    b. Charleston, S. C., September 24, 1794
    d. Charleston, S. C., February 3, 1863
    U. S. Representative, 1833-37

PINCKNEY, Thomas
    Federalist
    b. Charleston, S. C., October 23, 1750
    d. Charleston, S. C., November 2, 1828
    Governor of South Carolina, 1787-89
    U. S. Representative, 1797-1801

POINSETT, Joel Roberts
    Democrat
    b. Charleston, S. C., March 2, 1779
    d. near what is now Statesburg, S. C.,
        December 12, 1851
    U. S. Representative, 1821-25
    U. S. Secretary of War, 1837-41

POLLOCK, William Pegues
    Democrat
    b. near Cheraw, S. C., December 9, 1870
    d. Cheraw, S. C., June 2, 1922
    U. S. Senator, 1918-19

PRESTON, William Campbell
    Calhoun Nullifier
    b. Philadelphia, Pa., December 17, 1794
    d. Columbia, S. C., May 22, 1860
    U. S. Representative, 1833-42

RAGSDALE, James Willard
    Democrat
    b. Timmonsville, S. C., December 14, 1872
    d. Washington, D. C., July 23, 1919
    U. S. Representative, 1913-19

RAINEY, Joseph Hayne
    Republican
    b. Georgetown, S. C., June 21, 1832

d. Georgetown, S. C., August 2, 1887
U. S. Representative, 1870-79

RANSIER, Alonzo Jacob
    Republican
    b. Charleston, S. C., January 3, 1834
    d. Charleston, S. C., August 17, 1882
    U. S. Representative, 1873-75

READ, Jacob
    Federalist
    b. on Hobcaw Plantation, Christ Church Parish,
        near Charleston, S. C., 1751
    d. Charleston, S. C., July 17, 1816
    Member Continental Congress, 1783-85
    U. S. Senator, 1795-1801

RHETT, Robert Barnwell (formerly Robert Barn-
        well Smith)
    Democrat
    b. Beaufort, S. C., December 24, 1800
    d. St. James Parish, La., September 14, 1876
    U. S. Representative, 1837-49
    U. S. Senator, 1850-52

RICHARDS, James Prioleau
    Democrat
    b. Liberty, S. C., August 31, 1894
    U. S. Representative, 1933-57

RICHARDS, John Gardiner
    Democrat
    b. Liberty Hill, S. C., September 11, 1864
    d. ----
    Governor of South Carolina, 1927-31

RICHARDSON, John Peter
    State Rights Democrat
    b. Hickory Hill, S. C., April 14, 1801
    d. Fulton (later Pinewood), S. C., January 24, 1864
    U. S. Representative, 1836-39
    Governor of South Carolina, 1840-42

RICHARDSON, John P.
    Democrat
    Governor of South Carolina, 1886-90

RICHARDSON, John Smythe
    Democrat
    b. on Bloomhill Plantation, near Sumter,
        S. C., February 29, 1828
    d. at his country home "Shadyside," near
        Sumter, S. C., February 24, 1894

U. S. Representative, 1879-83

RILEY, Corinne Boyd
    Democrat
    b. Piedmont, S. C., July 4, 1894
    U. S. Representative, 1962-63

RILEY, John Jacob
    Democrat
    b. on a farm near Orangeburg, S. C., Febru-
        ary 1, 1895
    d. Surfside, near Myrtle Beach, S. C.,
        January 2, 1962
    U. S. Representative, 1945-49, 1951-62

RIVERS, Lucius Mendel
    Democrat
    b. Greenville, S. C., September 28, 1905
    d. Birmingham, Ala., December 28, 1970
    U. S. Representative, 1941-70

ROBERTSON, Thomas James
    Republican
    b. near Winnsboro, S. C., August 3, 1823
    d. Columbia, S. C., October 13, 1897
    U. S. Senator, 1868-77

ROGERS, James
    Democrat
    b. in what is now Goshen Hill Township,
        S. C., October 24, 1795
    d. South Carolina, December 12, 1873
    U. S. Representative, 1835-37, 1839-43

RUSSELL, Donald Stuart
    Democrat
    b. Lafayette Springs, Miss., February 22, 1906
    Governor of South Carolina, 1963-65
    U. S. Senator, 1965-66

RUTLEDGE, Edward
    Federalist
    b. Charlestown (now Charleston), S. C.,
        November 23, 1749
    d. Charleston, S. C., January 23, 1800
    Governor of South Carolina, 1798-1800

RUTLEDGE, John
    ----
    b. Charleston, S. C., September 1739
    d. Charleston, S. C., July 23, 1800
    Governor of South Carolina, 1779-82
    Associate Justice of the U. S. Supreme

Court, 1789-91

RUTLEDGE, John, Jr.
    Federalist
    b. Christ Church Parish, S. C., 1766
    d. Charleston, S. C., September 1, 1819
    U. S. Representative, 1797-1803

SAWYER, Frederick Adolphus
    Republican
    b. Bolton, Mass., December 12, 1822
    d. Shawnee, Tenn., July 31, 1891
    U. S. Senator, 1868-73

SCARBOROUGH, Robert Bethea
    Democrat
    b. Chesterfield, S. C., October 29, 1861
    d. Conway, S. C., November 23, 1927
    U. S. Representative, 1901-05

SCOTT, Robert K.
    Republican
    Governor of South Carolina, 1868-72

SEABROOK, Whitmarsh B.
    Democrat
    Governor of South Carolina, 1848-50

SHELL, George Washington
    Democrat
    b. near Laurens, S. C., November 13, 1831
    d. on his plantation, near Laurens, S. C.,
        December 15, 1899
    U. S. Representative, 1891-95

SHEPPARD, John Calhoun
    Democrat
    b. Edgefield County, S. C.
    d. October 17, 1931
    Governor of South Carolina, 1886

SIMKINS, Eldred
    Democrat
    b. Edgefield, S. C., August 30, 1779
    d. Edgefield, S. C., November 17, 1831
    U. S. Representative, 1818-21

SIMPSON, Richard Franklin
    Democrat
    b. Laurens, S. C., March 24, 1798
    d. Pendleton, S. C., October 28, 1882
    U. S. Representative, 1843-49

SIMPSON, William D.
    Democrat
    Governor of South Carolina, 1879-80

SIMS, Alexander Dromgoole
    Democrat
    b. near Randals Ordinary, Va., June 12, 1803
    d. Kingstree, S. C., November 22, 1848
    U. S. Representative, 1845-48

SIMS, Hugo Sheridan, Jr.
    Democrat
    b. Orangeburg, S. C., October 14, 1921
    U. S. Representative, 1949-51

SINGLETON, Thomas Day
    Nullifier
    b. near Kingstree, S. C.
    d. en route to Washington, D. C., November
       25, 1833
    U. S. Representative, 1833

SMALLS, Robert
    Republican
    b. Beaufort, S. C., April 5, 1839
    d. Beaufort, S. C., February 22, 1915
    U. S. Representative, 1875-79, 1882-83, 1884-87

SMITH, Charles A.
    Democrat
    Governor of South Carolina, 1915

SMITH, Ellison DuRant
    Democrat
    b. Lynchburg, S. C., August 1, 1866
    d. Lynchburg, S. C., November 17, 1944
    U. S. Senator, 1909-44

SMITH, O'Brien
    ----
    b. Ireland, about 1756
    d. South Carolina, April 27, 1811
    U. S. Representative, 1805-07

SMITH, William
    Democrat
    b. South Carolina, 1762
    d. at his estate "Calhoun Place," on Mays-
      ville Pike, S. C., June 26, 1840
    U. S. Senator, 1816-23, 1826-31

SMITH, William
    ----

b. Bucks County, Pa., September 20, 1751
d. Spartan District, S. C., June 22, 1837
U. S. Representative, 1797-99

SMITH, William Loughton
   Federalist
   b. Charleston, S. C., 1758
   d. Charleston, S. C., December 19, 1812
   U. S. Representative, 1789-97

STACKHOUSE, Eli Thomas
   Democrat
   b. Little Rock, S. C., March 27, 1824
   d. Washington, D. C., June 14, 1892
   U. S. Representative, 1891=92

STEVENSON, William Francis
   Democrat
   b. in what is now Loray, near Statesville,
        N. C., November 23, 1861
   d. Washington, D. C., February 12, 1942
   U. S. Representative, 1917-33

STOKES, James William
   Democrat
   b. near Orangeburg, S. C., December 12, 1853
   d. Orangeburg, S. C., July 6, 1901
   U. S. Representative, 1895-96, 1896-1901

STRAIT, Thomas Jefferson
   Alliance Democrat
   b. Chester District, S. C., December 25, 1846
   d. Lancaster, S. C., April 18, 1924
   U. S. Representative, 1893-99

SUMTER, Thomas
   Democrat
   b. Hanover County, Va., August 14, 1734
   d. on his plantation "South Mount," near
        Statesburg, S. C., June 1, 1832
   U. S. Representative, 1789-93, 1797-1801
   U. S. Senator, 1801-1810

SUMTER, Thomas De Lage
   Democrat
   b. Germantown, Pa., November 14, 1809
   d. on his plantation "South Mount," near
        Statesburg, S. C., July 2, 1874
   U. S. Representative, 1839-43

TALBERT, Jasper William
   Democrat
   b. near Edgefield, S. C., October 6, 1846

d. Greenwood, S. C., February 5, 1931
U. S. Representative, 1893-1903

TAYLOR, John
Democrat
b. near Granby, S. C., May 4, 1770
d. Camden, S. C., April 16, 1832
U. S. Representative, 1807-10
U. S. Senator, 1810-16
Governor of South Carolina, 1826-28

TAYLOR
John
U. S. Representative, 1815-17

TAYLOR, John Clarence
Democrat
b. Honea Path, S. C., March 2, 1890
U. S. Representative, 1933-39

THOMPSON, Hugh Smith
Democrat
Governor of South Carolina, 1882-86

THOMPSON, Waddy, Jr.
Whig
b. Pickensville (now Pickens), S. C.,
    January 8, 1798
d. Tallahassee, Fla., November 23, 1868
U. S. Representative, 1835-41

THURMOND, James Strom
Republican
b. Edgefield, S. C., December 5, 1902
Governor of South Carolina, 1947-51
U. S. Senator, 1954-56, 1956-64 (Democrat),
    1964- (Republican)

TILLMAN, Benjamin Ryun
Democrat
b. near Trenton, S. C., August 11, 1847
d. Washington, D. C., July 3, 1918
Governor of South Carolina, 1890-94
U. S. Senator, 1895-1918

TILLMAN, George Dionysius
Democrat
b. near Curryton, S. C., August 21, 1826
d. Clarks Hill, S. C., February 2, 1902
U. S. Representative, 1879-82, 1883-93

TIMMERMAN, George Bell, Jr.
    Democrat
    b. Edgefield County, S. C., March 28, 1881
    d. April 1966
    Governor of South Carolina, 1955-59

TROTTI, Samuel Wilds
    ----
    b. Barnwell, S. C., July 18, 1810
    d. Buckhead, S. C., June 24, 1856
    U. S. Representative, 1842-43

TUCKER, Starling
    ----
    b. Halifax County, S. C., 1770
    d. Mountain Shoals (now Enoree), S. C.,
        January 3, 1834
    U. S. Representative, 1817-31

TUCKER, Thomas Tudor
    Federalist
    b. Port Royal, Bermuda, June 25, 1745
    d. Washington, D. C., May 2, 1828
    Member Continental Congress, 1787-88
    U. S. Representative, 1789-93

WALLACE, Alexander Stuart
    Republican
    b. near York, S. C., December 30, 1810
    d. near York, S. C., June 27, 1893
    U. S. Representative, 1870-77

WALLACE, Daniel
    Whig
    b. near Laurens, S. C., May 9, 1801
    d. Jonesville, S. C., May 13, 1859
    U. S. Representative, 1848-53

WATSON, Albert William
    Republican
    b. Sumter, S. C., August 30, 1922
    U. S. Representative, 1963-65 (Democrat),
        1965-71 (Republican)

WEST, John Carl
    Democrat
    b. Camden, S. C., August 27, 1922
    Governor of South Carolina, 1971-75

WHALEY, Richard Smith
    Democrat
    b. Charleston, S. C., July 15, 1874
    d. Charleston, S. C., November 8, 1951

U. S. Representative, 1913-21

WHITTEMORE, Benjamin Franklin
    Republican
    b. Malden, Mass., May 18, 1824
    d. Montvale, a suburb of Woburn, Mass.,
        January 25, 1894
    U. S. Representative, 1868-70

WILLIAMS, David Rogerson
    Democrat
    b. Robbins Neck, S. C., March 8, 1776
    d. accidentally while superintending con-
        struction of a bridge over Lynch's Creek,
        on the road to Georgetown, S. C., No-
        vember 17, 1830
    U. S. Representative, 1805-09, 1811-13
    Governor of South Carolina, 1814-16

WILLIAMS, Ransome Judson
    Democrat
    b. Cope, S. C., January 4, 1892
    d. January 1970
    Governor of South Carolina, 1945-47

WILSON, John
    ----
    b. at Wilson's Ferry (now Pelzer), S. C.,
        August 11, 1773
    d. near Golden Grove, S. C., August 13, 1828
    U. S. Representative, 1821-27

WILSON, John Lyde
    Democrat-Republican
    Governor of South Carolina, 1822-24

WILSON, Stanyarne
    Democrat
    b. Yorkville (now York), S. C., January 10, 1860
    d. Spartanburg, S. C., February 14, 1928
    U. S. Representative, 1895-1901

WINN, Richard
    Democrat
    b. Fauquier County, Va., 1750
    d. on his plantation at Duck River, Tenn.,
        December 19, 1818
    U. S. Representative, 1793-97, 1803-13

WITHERSPOON, Robert
    Democrat
    b. near Kingstree, S. C., January 29, 1767
    d. near Maysville, S. C., October 11, 1837

U. S. Representative, 1809-11

WOFFORD, Thomas Albert
    Democrat
    b. Madden Station, S. C., September 27, 1908
    U. S. Senator, 1956

WOODWARD, Joseph Addison
    Democrat
    b. Winnsboro, S. C., April 11, 1806
    d. Talladega, Ala., August 3, 1885
    U. S. Representative, 1943-53

WOODWARD, William

    U. S. Representative, 1815-17

PROMINENT PERSONALITIES

The following select list of prominent persons of
South Carolina has been selected to indicate the valuable contributions they have made to American life.

BARUCH, Bernard Mannes
    b. August 19, 1870
    d. June 20, 1965
    Appointed to Advisory Commission of Council
        for National Defense, 1916
    Chairman, Committee on raw materials,
        minerals and metals, 1918-19
    Appointed to Atomic Energy Committee of United
        Nations, 1946
    Author: <u>Making of Economic and Reparation
        Sections of Peace Treaty</u>, 1920
           <u>Baruch: My Own Story</u>, 1957

CLARK, Mark W.
    b. Madison Barracks, N. Y., May 1, 1896
    Graduate U. S. Military Academy, 1917
    Lieutenant General, U. S. Army, 1942
    Commander of U. S. 5th Army, North Africa
        and Italy, 1943-44
    General, U. S. Army, 1945
    Chief U. S. Forces, Austria, 1945-47
    Commander-in-chief, United Nations Command,
        Korea
    President, The Citadel Military College, S. C.,
        1954-66

COKER, David R.
    b. Hartsville, S. C., November 20, 1870
    d. November 28, 1938
    Originator, varieties of staple cotton
    President, J. L. Coker and Co., merchants
    Member National Agricultural Commission to
        Europe, 1918

GADSDEN, Christopher
    b. Charleston, S. C., February 16, 1724
    d. August 28, 1805
    Member Continental Congress, 1774-76
    Brigadier General, Continental Army, 1776-78
    Member S. C. Convention for ratification of
        U. S. Constitution

GADSDEN, James
    b. Charleston, S. C., May 15, 1788
    d. December 26, 1858
    Member first Florida legislative council,
        1824
    President Louisville, Cincinnati and Charles-
        ton Railroad, 1849-50
    Negotiated Treaty for purchase of strip of
        territory from Mexico in what is now

New Mexico and Arizona - Gadsden Purchase
U. S. Minister to Mexico, 1853-54

GREGG, William
    b. Carmichaels, W. Va., February 3, 1800
    d. Kalmia, S. C., September 13, 1877
    Jewelry business
    Cotton manufacturer - wrote essays which
        advocated development of new economic
        basis for south based on cotton manufac-
        turing

HEYWARD, DuBose
    b. Charleston, S. C., August 31, 1885
    d. July 16, 1940
    Author: Skylines and Horizons, 1924
        Porgy, 1925
        Angel, 1926
        Marriba's Daughters, 1929
        Half Pint Flask, 1929
        Porgy - dramatized in collaboration
    with Dorothy Heyward, 1927 - play pro-
    duced, 1931
        Porgy and Bess - opera with George
    Gershwin, produced 1935

JACKSON, Andrew
    b. Waxhaw, S. C., March 15, 1767
    d. "Hermitage," near Nashville, Tenn.,
        June 8, 1845
    U. S. Representative (Tennessee), 1796-97
    U. S. Senator (Tennessee), 1797-98
    Major general U. S. Army, 1814 -
        defeated British, Battle of New Orleans,
        January 8, 1815
    First governor Florida Territory, 1821
    U. S. Senator, 1823-25
    7th President of the United States, 1829-37

LONGSTREET, James
    b. Edgefield District, S. C., January 8,
        1821
    d. Gainesville, Ga., 1904
    Lieutenant General, Confederate Army,
        1862
    Surrendered with General Robert E. Lee,
        Appomatox Court House, 1865
    U. S. Minister to Turkey, 1880-81
    U. S. Marshal, 1881-84
    U. S. Railroad Commissioner, 1898-1904

MARION, Francis
    b. Berkeley County, S. C., 1732

d. St. John's Parish, S. C., February 27,
    1795
Member South Carolina Provincial Congress
    from St. John's Parish, 1775
Commander of only Revolutionary forces
    in South Carolina, 1780-81
Member South Carolina Senate, 1781, 1782, 1784
Member South Carolina Constitutional
    Convention, 1790
Member South Carolina Senate, 1791

MILLS, Robert
    b. Charleston, S. C., August 12, 1781
    d, March 3, 1855
Architect of public buildings, Washington,
    D. C.
Designer, Treasury Building, General Post
    Office, Patent Office Building, Washing-
    ton Monument

PETERKIN, Julia Mood
    b. Laurens County, S. C., October 31, 1880
    d. South Carolina, August 10, 1961
    Author: <u>Green Thursday</u>, 1924
            <u>Black April</u>, 1927
            <u>Sister Mary</u> (awarded Pulitzer Prize
        of $1,000), 1928
            <u>Bright Skin</u>, 1932
            <u>Roll, Jordan, Roll</u>, 1933
            <u>Plantation Christmas</u>, 1934

PETIGRU, James Louis
    b. Abbeville, District, S. C., May 10,
        1789
    d. Charleston, S. C., March 9, 1863
Attorney general, South Carolina, 1822
Member South Carolina legislature, 1830
    leader of anti-nullificationist
    forces

PINCKNEY, Charles Coatesworth
    b. Charlestown (now Charleston), S. C.,
        February 25, 1746
    d. Charleston, S. C., August 16, 1825
Served in Revolutionary War at battles
of Germantown and Brandywine, 1777
Member South Carolina Convention to ratify
    U. S. Constitution, 1788
U. S. Minister to France, 1796 - French
    Directory would not recognize his status
Appointed representative along with John
    Marshall and Elbridge Gerry to France
    to negotiate XYZ Affair

SIMMS, William Gilmore
 b. Charleston, S. C., April 17, 1806
 d. Charleston, S. C., June 11, 1870
 Editor, Charleston City <u>Gazette</u>, c. 1828
 Opposed doctrine of nullification
 Author: <u>Guy Rivers</u>, 1834
    <u>Yemasse</u>, 1835
    <u>The Partisan</u>, 1835
    <u>Mellichampe</u>, 1836
    <u>Beauchampe</u>, 1842
    <u>Katharine Walton</u>, 1851

SULLY, Thomas
 b. Horncastle, England, June 8, 1783
 d. Philadelphia, Pa., November 5, 1872
 Recognized as leading portrait painter in
  United States after 1827
 Portraits: Washington Irving
    Queen Victoria
    Rembrandt Peale
    Lafayette
    Washington Crossing the Delaware
    The Capture of Major Andre

TIMROD, Henry
 b. Charleston, S. C., December 8, 1828
 d. Columbia, S. C., October 6, 1867
 Poet - gained fame as Laureate of the
  Confederacy
 Poems: "Charleston"
   "The Cotton-Boll"
   "Katie"
   "A Cry to Arms:
   "Carolina"
   "Magnolia Cemetery"

TOWNES, Charles H.
 b. Greenville, S. C., July 28, 1915
 Physicist
 Vice President, director Institute for Defense
  Analyses, Washington, 1959-61
 Awarded Nobel Prize for Physics, 1964

FIRST STATE CONSTITUTION

CONSTITUTION OF SOUTH CAROLINA—1776 * a

Whereas the British Parliament, claiming of late years a right to bind the North American colonies by law in all cases whatsoever, have enacted statutes for raising a revenue in those colonies and disposing of such revenue as they thought proper, without the consent and against the will of the colonists. And whereas it appearing to them that (they not being represented in Parliament) such claim was altogether unconstitutional, and, if admitted, would at once reduce them from the rank of freemen to a state of the most abject slavery; the said colonies, therefore, severally remonstrated against the passing, and petitioned for the repeal, of those acts, but in vain; and whereas the said claim being persisted in, other unconstitutional and oppressive statutes have been since enacted by which the powers of admiralty courts in the colonies are extended beyond their ancient limits, and jurisdiction is given to such courts in cases similar to those which in Great Britain are triable by jury; persons are liable to be sent to and tried in Great Britain for an offence created and made capital by one of those statutes, though committed in the colonies; the harbor of Boston was blocked up; people indicted for murder in the Massachusetts Bay may, at the will of a governor, be sent for trial to any other colony, or even to Great Britain; the chartered constitution of government in that colony is materially altered; the English laws and a free government, to which the inhabitants of Quebec were entitled by the King's royal proclamation, are abolished and French laws are restored; the Roman Catholic religion (although before tolerated and freely exercised there) and an absolute government are established in that province, and its limits extended through a vast tract of country so as to border on the free Protestant English settlements, with design of using a whole people

* Verified by—"Constitution" in "The Statutes at Large of South Carolina. Edited by Thomas Cooper, M. D.; LL. D. Vol. I. Columbia, S. C. 1836" pp. 128–134.

a This constitution was framed by the "Provincial Congress" of South Carolina, and adopted March 26, 1776. It was not submitted to the people for ratification.

differing in religious principles from the neighboring colonies, and subject to arbitrary power, as fit instruments to overawe and subdue the colonies. And whereas the delegates of all the colonies on this continent, from Nova Scotia to Georgia, assembled in a general Congress at Philadelphia, in the most dutiful manner laid their complaints at the foot of the throne, and humbly implored their sovereign that his royal authority and interposition might be used for their relief from the grievances occasioned by those statutes, and assured His Majesty that harmony between Great Britain and America, ardently desired by the latter, would be thereby immediately restored, and that the colonists confided in the magnanimity and justice of the King and Parliament for redress of the many other grievances under which they labored. And whereas these complaints being wholly disregarded, statutes still more cruel than those above mentioned have been enacted, prohibiting the intercourse of the colonies with each other, restricting their trade, and depriving many thousands of people of the means of subsistence, by restraining them from fishing on the American coast. And whereas large fleets and armies having been sent to America in order to enforce the execution of those laws, and to compel an absolute and implicit submission to the will of a corrupt and despotic administration, and in consequence thereof, hostilities having been commenced in the Massachusetts Bay, by the troops under command of General Gage, whereby a number of peaceable, helpless, and unarmed people were wantonly robbed and murdered, and there being just reason to apprehend that like hostilities would be committed in all the other colonies. The colonists were therefore driven to the necessity of taking up arms, to repel force by force, and to defend themselves and their properties against lawless invasions and depredations. Nevertheless, the delegates of the said colonies assembled in another Congress at Philadelphia, anxious to procure a reconciliation with Great Britain upon just and constitutional principles, supplicated His Majesty to direct some mode by which the united applications of his faithful colonists might be improved into a happy and permanent reconciliation, that in the mean time measures might be taken for preventing the further destruction of their lives, and that such statutes as immediately distressed any of the colonists might be repealed. And whereas, instead of obtaining that justice, to which the colonists were and are of right entitled, the unnatural civil war into which they were thus precipitated and are involved, hath been prosecuted with unremitted violence, and the governors and others bearing the royal commission in the colonies having broken the most solemn promises and engagements, and violated every obligation of honor, justice, and humanity, have caused the persons of divers good people to be seized and imprisoned, and their properties to be forcibly taken and detained, or destroyed, without any crime or forfeiture; excited domestic insurrections; proclaimed freedom to servants and slaves, enticed or stolen them from, and armed them against their masters; instigated and encouraged the Indian nations to war against the colonies; dispensed with the law of the land, and substituted the law martial in its stead; killed many of the colonists; burned several towns, and threatened to burn the rest, and daily endeavor by a conduct which has sullied the British arms, and would disgrace even savage nations, to effect the ruin and destruction of the colonies; and whereas a statute hath been lately passed, whereby, under pretence that the said colonies are in open rebellion, all trade and commerce whatsoever with them is prohibited; vessels belonging to their inhabitants trading in, to, or from the said colonies, with the cargoes and effects on board such vessels, are made lawful prize, and the masters and crews of such vessels are subjected by force to act on board the King's ships against their country and dearest friends; and all seizures and detention or destruction of the persons and properties of the colonists which have at any time been made or committed for withstanding or suppressing the said pretended rebellion, and which shall be made in pursuance of the said act, or for the service of the public, are justified, and persons suing for damages in such cases are, on failing in their suits, subjected to payment of very heavy expenses. And whereas large reënforcements of troops and ships have been ordered and are daily expected in America for carrying on war against each of the united colonies by the most vigorous exertions. And whereas in consequence of a plan recommended by the governors, and which seems to have been concerted between them and their ministerial masters to withdraw the usual officers and thereby loosen the bands of government and create anarchy and confusion in the colonies. Lord William Campbell, late governor, on the fifteenth day of September last, dissolved the general assembly of this colony, and no other hath been since called, although by law the sitting and holding of general assemblies cannot be intermitted above six months, and having used his utmost efforts to destroy the lives, liberties, and properties of the good people here, whom by the duty of his station he was bound to protect, withdrew himself from the colony and carried off the great seal and the royal instructions to governors. And whereas the judges of courts of law here have refused to exercise their respective functions, so that it is become indispensably necessary that during the present situation of American affairs, and until an accommodation of the unhappy differences between Great Britain and America can be obtained, (an event which, though traduced and treated as rebels, we still earnestly desire,) some mode should be established by common consent, and for the good of the people, the origin and end of all governments, for regulating the internal polity of this colony. The congress being vested with powers competent for the purpose, and having fully deliberated touching the premises, do therefore resolve:

I. That this congress being a full and free representation of the people of this colony, shall henceforth be deemed and called the general assembly of South Carolina, and as such shall continue until the twenty-first day of October next, and no longer.

II. That the general assembly shall, out of their own body, elect by ballot a legislative council, to consist of thirteen members, (seven of whom shall be a quorum,) and to continue for the same time as the general assembly.

III. That the general assembly and the said legislative council shall jointly choose by ballot from among themselves, or from the people at large, a president and commander-in-chief and a vice-president of the colony.

IV. That a member of the general assembly being chosen and acting as president and commander-in-chief, or vice-president, or one of the legislative council shall vacate his seat in the general assembly and another person shall be elected in his room; and if one of the legislative council is chosen president and commander-in-chief or vice-president, he shall lose his seat and another person shall be elected in his stead.

V. That there be a privy council, whereof the vice-president of the colony shall of course be a member and president of the privy council, and that six other members be chosen by ballot, three by the general assembly, and three by the legislative council: *Provided always*, That no officer in the army or navy in the service of the continent, or of this colony, shall be eligible. And a member of the general assembly, or of the legislative council, being chosen of the privy council, shall not thereby lose his seat in the general assembly, or in the legislative council, unless he be elected vice-president of the colony, in which case he shall, and another person shall be chosen in his stead. The privy council (of which four to be a quorum) to advise the president and commander-in-chief when required, but he shall not be bound to consult them, unless in cases after mentioned.

VI. That the qualifications of president and commander-in-chief, and vice-president of the colony, and members of the legislative and privy council, shall be the same as of members of the general assembly, and on being elected they shall take an oath of qualification in the general assembly.

VII. That the legislative authority be vested in the president and commander-in-chief, the general assembly and legislative council. All money-bills for the support of government shall originate in the general assembly, and shall not be altered or amended by the legislative council, but may be rejected by them. All other bills and ordinances may take rise in the general assembly or legislative council, and may be altered, amended, or rejected by either. Bills having passed the general assembly and legislative council may be assented to or rejected by the president and commander-in-chief. Having received his assent, they shall have all the force and validity of an act of general assembly of this colony. And the general assembly and legislative council, respectively, shall enjoy all other privileges which have at any time been claimed or exercised by the commons house of assembly, but the legislative council shall have no power of expelling their own members.

VIII. That the general assembly and legislative council may adjourn themselves respectively, and the president and commander-in-chief shall have no power to adjourn, prorogue, or dissolve them, but may. if necessary, call them before the time to which they shall stand adjourned. And where a bill has been rejected, it may, on a meeting after adjournment of not less than three days of the general assembly and legislative council, be brought in again.

IX. That the general assembly and legislative council shall each choose their respective speakers and their own officers without control.

X. That if a member of the general assembly or of the legislative council shall accept any place of emolument or any commission, except in the militia, he shall vacate his seat, and there shall thereupon be a new election, but he shall not be disqualified from serving upon being reëlected.

XI. That on the last Monday in October next, and the day following, and on the same days of every second year thereafter, members of the general assembly shall be chosen, to meet on the first Monday in December then next, and continue for two years from the said last Monday in October. The general assembly to consist of the same number of members as this congress does, each parish and district having the same representation as at present, viz: the parish of Saint Philip and Saint Michael, Charlestown, thirty members; the parish of Christ Church, six members; the parish of Saint John, in Berkely County, six members; the parish of Saint Andrew, six members; the parish of Saint George Dorchester, six members; the parish of Saint James Goose Creek, six members; the parish of Saint Thomas and Saint Dennis, six members; the parish of Saint Paul, six members; the parish of Saint Bartholemew, six members; the parish of Saint Helena, six members; the parish of Saint James Santee, six members; the parish of Prince George, Winyaw, six members; the parish of Prince Frederick, six members; the parish of Saint John, in Colleton County, six members; the parish of Saint Peter, six members; the parish of Prince William, six members; the parish of Saint Stephen, six members; the district to the eastward of Wateree River, ten members; the district of Ninety-six, ten members; the district of Saxe Gotha, six members; the district between Broad and Saluda Rivers, in three divisions, viz: the Lower district, four members; the Little River district, four members; the Upper or Spartan district, four members; the district between Broad and Catawba Rivers, ten members; the district called the New Acquisition, ten members; the parish of Saint Mathew, six members; the parish of Saint David, six members; the district between Savannah River and the North Fork of Edisto, six members. And the election of the said members shall be conducted as near as may be agreeable to the directions of the election act, and where there are no churches or church wardens in a district or parish, the general assembly, at some convenient time before their expiration, shall appoint places of election and persons to receive votes and make returns. The qualifications of electors shall be the same as required by law, but persons having property, which, according to the rate of the last preceding tax, is taxable at the sums mentioned in the election act, shall be entitled to vote, though it was no actually taxed, having the other qualifications mentioned in that act; electors shall take an oath of qualification, if required by the returning-officer. The qualification of the elected to be the same as mentioned in the election act, and construed to mean clear of debt.

XII. That if any parish or district neglects or refuses to elect members, or if the members chosen do not meet in general assembly, those who do meet shall have the powers of a general assembly; not less than forty-nine members shall make a house to do business, but the speaker or any seven members may adjourn from day to day.

XIII. That as soon as may be, after the first meeting of the general assembly, a president and commander-in-chief, a vice-president of the colony and privy council, shall be chosen in manner and for the time above mentioned, and till such choice be made the former president and commander-in-chief and vice-president of the colony and privy council shall continue to act as such.

XIV. That in case of the death of the president and commander-in-chief, or his absence from the colony, the vice-president of the colony shall succeed to his office, and the privy council shall choose out of their own body a vice-president of the colony, and in case of the death of the vice-president of the colony, or his absence from the colony, one of the privy council (to be chosen by themselves) shall succeed to his office, until a nomination to those offices, respectively, by the general assembly and legislative council for the remainder of the time for which the officer so dying or being absent was appointed.

XV. That the delegates of this colony in the Continental Congress be chosen by the general assembly and legislative council jointly by ballot in the general assembly.

XVI. That the vice-president of the colony and the privy council, or the vice-president and a majority of the privy council for the time being, shall exercise the powers of a court of chancery, and there shall be an ordinary who shall exercise the powers heretofore exercised by that officer in this colony.

XVII. That the jurisdiction of the court of admiralty be confined to maritime causes.

XVIII. That all suits and process depending in any court of law or equity may, if either party shall be so inclined, be proceeded in and continued to a final ending, without being obliged to commence *de novo*. And the judges of the courts of law shall cause jury-lists to be made, and juries to be summoned, as near as may be, according to the directions of the acts of the general assembly in such cases provided.

XIX. That justices of the peace shall be nominated by the general assembly and commissioned by the president and commander-in-chief, during pleasure. They shall not be entitled to fees except on prosecutions for felony, and not acting in the magistracy, they shall not be entitled to the privileges allowed to them by law.

XX. That all other judicial officers shall be chosen by ballot, jointly by the general assembly and legislative council, and except the judges of the court of chancery, commissioned by the president and commander-in-chief, during good behavior, but shall be removed on address of the general assembly and legislative council.

XXI. That sheriffs, qualified as by law directed, shall be chosen in like manner by the general assembly and legislative council, and commissioned by the president and commander-in-chief, for two years only.

XXII. That the commissioners of the treasury, the secretary of the colony, register of mesne conveyances, attorney-general, and powder-receiver, be chosen by the general assembly and legislative council, jointly by ballot, and commissioned by the president and commander-in-chief during good behavior, but shall be removed on address of the general assembly and legislative council.

XXIII. That all field-officers in the army, and all captains in the navy, shall be, by the general assembly and legislative council, chosen jointly by ballot, and commissioned by the president and commander-in-chief, and that all other officers in the army or navy shall be commissioned by the president and commander-in-chief.

XXIV. That in case of vacancy in any of the offices above directed to be filled by the general assembly and legislative council, the president and commander-in-chief, with the advice and consent of the privy council, may appoint others in their stead, until there shall be an election by the general assembly and legislative council to fill their vacancies respectively.

XXV. That the president and commander-in-chief, with the advice and consent of the privy council, may appoint during pleasure, until otherwise directed by resolution of the general assembly and legislative council, all other necessary officers, except such as are by law directed to be otherwise chosen.

XXVI. That the president and commander-in-chief shall have no power to make war or peace, or enter into any final treaty, without the consent of the general assembly and legislative council.

XXVII. That if any parish or district shall neglect to elect a member or members on the day of election, or in case any person chosen a member of the general assembly shall refuse to qualify and take his seat as such, or die or depart the colony, the said general assembly shall appoint proper days for electing a member or members of the said general assembly in such cases respectively; and on the death of a member of the legislative or privy council, another member shall be chosen in his room, in manner above mentioned, for the election of members of the legislative and privy council respectively.

XXVIII. That the resolutions of the Continental Congress, now of force in this colony, shall so continue until altered or revoked by them.

XXIX. That the resolutions of this or any former congress of this colony, and all laws now of force here, (and not hereby altered,) shall so continue until altered or repealed by the legislature of this colony, unless where they are temporary, in which case they shall expire at the times respectively limited for their duration.

XXX. That the executive authority be vested in the president and commander-in-chief, limited and restrained as aforesaid.

XXXI. That the president and commander-in-chief, the vice-president of the colony, and privy council, respectively, shall have the same personal privileges as are allowed by act of assembly to the governor, lieutenant-governor, and privy council.

XXXII. That all persons now in office shall hold their commissions until there shall be a new appointment in manner above directed, at which time all commissions not derived from authority of the congress of this colony shall cease and be void

XXXIII. That all persons who shall be chosen and appointed to any office or to any place of trust, before entering upon the execution of office, shall take the following oath: " I, A. B., do swear that I will, to the utmost of my power, support, maintain, and defend the constitution of South Carolina, as established by Congress on the twenty-sixth day of March, one thousand seven hundred and seventy-six, until an accommodation of the differences between Great Britain and America shall take place, or I shall be released from this oath by the legislative authority of the said colony: So help me God." And all such persons shall also take an oath of office.

XXXIV. That the following yearly salaries be allowed to the public officers undermentioned: The president and commander-in-chief, nine thousand pounds; the chief justice and the assistant judges, the salaries, respectively, as by act of assembly established; the attorney-general, two thousand one hundred pounds, in lieu of all charges against the public for fees upon criminal prosecutions; the ordinary, one thousand pounds; the three commissioners of the treasury, two thousand pounds each; and all other public officers shall have the

same salaries as are allowed such officers, respectively, by act of assembly.

By order of the congress, March 26, 1776.

WILLIAM HENRY DRAYTON, *President.*

Attested:

PETER TIMOTHY, *Secretary.*

SELECTED DOCUMENTS

The documents selected for this section have been
chosen to reflect the interests or attitudes of the
contemporary observer or writer. Documents relating
specifically to the constitutional development of South
Carolina will be found in volume eight of <u>Sources and
Documents of United States Constitutions</u>, a companion
reference collection to the Columbia University volumes
previously cited.

SEVENTEENTH CENTURY VIEWS OF SOUTH CAROLINA

The following letters of Thomas
Newe present an interesting account of South Carolina in 1682.

Source: J. Franklin Jameson, ed. <u>Original Narratives</u>
<u>of Early American History</u>. Alexander S. Salley, Jr.,
ed. <u>Narratives of Early Carolina, 1650-1708</u>.
New York: Charles Scribner's Sons, 1911, 181-87.

May the 17th, 1682, from CHARLES TOWN on
Ashley River by way of Barbadoes in the
Samuel.

Most Honourd Father:

THE 12th of this instant by the providence of God after a
long and tedious passage we came to an Anchor against Charles
town at 10 in the night in $3\frac{1}{2}$ fathom water, on the sixth we
made land 60 miles to the South of Ashley River against which
we came the 8 but could not get in by reason of contrary winds
sooner then we did. We had little or nothing observable in
the whole voyage, but the almost continual S.W. winds. God
be thanked I had my health very well except a day or two of
Sea sickness but most of the other passengers were much
troubled with the scurvy; Of 62 that came out of England we
lost 3, two of them were seamen, one dyed of the scurvey, the
other fell overboard, the third was a woman in child bed, her
child died shortly after her. As for the Countrey I can say
but little of it as yet on my one [own] knowledge, but what I
hear from others. The Town which two years since had but
3 or 4 houses, hath now about a hundred houses in it, all
which are wholy built of wood, tho here is excellent Brick
made, but little of it. All things are very dear in the Town;
milk 2 *d* a quart, beefe 4 *d* a pound, pork 3 *d*, but far better
then our English, the common drink of the Countrey is Molos-
sus and water, I don't hear of any mault that is made hear as
yet. The English Barly and Wheat do thrive very well, but
the Indian corn being more hearty and profitable, the other is
not much regarded. I am told that there is great plenty of
all things in the Countrey, whither I intend to go as soon as
conveniently I can dispose of my goods, which I fear will not

be soon, nor to such advantage as we expected.[1] Severall in the Country have great stocks of Cattle and they sell so well to new comers that they care not for killing, which is the reason provision is so dear in the Town, whilst they in the Country are furnisht with Venison, fish, and fowle by the Indians for trifles, and they that understand it make as good butter and cheese as most in England. The land near the sea side is generally a light and sandy ground, but up in the Country they say there is very good land, and the farther up the better, but that which at present doth somewhat hinder the selling [settling] farther up, is a war that they are ingaged in against a tribe of Barbarous Indians being not above 60 in number, but by reason of their great growth and cruelty in feeding on all their neighbours, they are terrible to all other Indians, of which, there are above 40 severall Kingdoms, the strength and names of them all being known to our Governer who upon any occasion summons their Kings in. We are at peace with all but those common enemies of mankind, those man eaters before mentioned, by name the Westos,[2] who have lately killed two eminent planters that lived far up in the Country, so that they are resolved now if they can find their settlement (which they often change) to cut them all off. There is a small party of English out after them, and the most potent Kingdome of the Indians armed by us and continually in pursuit of them. When we came into Ashley river we found six small vessels in the Harbour, but great ones may and have come in by the assistance of a good Pilot, and if they can make good wine hear, which they have great hopes of, and this year will be the time of tryall which if it hits no doubt but the place will flourish exceedingly, but if the vines do not prosper I question whither it will ever be any great place of trade. On Sunday the 14th of this instant a small vessell that came from Mewis[3] hither, was cast away upon the Bar, but the men and

---

[1] He evidently expected to do as many of the foremost men of South Carolina had done and as many more of them subsequently did. They accumulated capital in trade and then took up planting and grew wealthy thereby.

[2] See Woodward's *Westoe Voiage*, pp. 130-134, *supra*, for an account of the Westoes. They rose against the English settlements in 1673, 1680, and 1681, but were defeated each time. See *Collections of the South Carolina Historical Society*, V. 461; *Calendar of State Papers, Colonial*, 1681-1685, pp. 508-510.

[3] Nevis.

goods were all saved. This is the first opportunity I have had
to write since I came from England but I hope to find more
opportunityes here, then I had at Sea, this with my most
humble duty to yourself and my Mother, my kind love to my
sister and Brothers being all from

Your most duetifull and obedient son
Thomas Newe

My duty to my Grandmother and my love to all my relations and friends that enquire concerning me.

May 29th, 1682, by way of
Barbados.

Most Honoured Father:

The 17th of this Instant by way of Barbados in the *Samuel*,
being the 1ʳˢᵗ opportunity since my departure from England,
I sent you a letter wherein I gave you an account of our safe
arrival, but not of the Voyage, that I leave to my Journall
which I intend to send by the first Ship that goes directly for
England, with my knowledge of the Countrey of which I have
not seen much yet, but one thing I understand (to my sorrow)
that I knew not before, the most have a seasoning, but few
dye of it. I find the Commonalty here to be mightily dissatis-
fied, the reason is 3 or 4 of the great ones, for furs and skins,
have furnished the Indians with arms and ammunitions
especially those with whome they are now at War, for from
those they had all or most of their fur, so that trade which 3
or 4 only kept in their hands is at present gone to decay, and
now they have armed the next most potent tribe of the Indians to fight the former, and some few English there are out,
looking after them, which is a charge to the people and a stop
[to] the further setling of the Countrey.¹ The Soyl is gen-

¹ Dr. Henry Woodward had built up a fine trade with the Westo Indians,
in which he was personally interested. In 1680 the Savannah Indians pushed
eastward from their towns near the Gulf, west of the Appalachicola River, to
the Westoboo (Savannah). In the same year, the Westoes, in violation of a
treaty they had made with the governor, killed, or captured for slaves, some
Indians of the coastal tribes near Charles Town, and war was declared upon
them by the whites. Dr. Woodward was accused of having furnished the Westoes
with arms to use against the friendly Indians and prohibited from trading or
negotiating with them. He was subsequently fined for his conduct, but the

erally very light, but apt to produce whatsoever is put into it. There are already all sorts of English fruit and garden herbs besides many others that I never saw in England, and they do send a great deal of Pork, Corn and Cedar to Barbados, besides the victualling of severall Vessels that come in here, as Privateers and others which to do in the space of 12 years the time from the 1ᵐᵗ seating of it by the English, is no small work, especially if we consider the first Planters which were most of them tradesmen, poor and wholy ignorant of husbandry and till of late but few in number, it being encreased more the 3 or 4 last years then the whole time before, the whole at presen[t] not amounting to 4000,[1] so that their whole Business was to clear a little ground to get Bread for their Familyes, few of them having wherewithall to purchase a Cow, the first stock whereof they were furnished with, from Bermudas and New England, from the later of which they had their horses which are not so good as those in England, but by reason of their scarcity much dearer, an ordinary Colt at 3 years old being valued at 15 or 16 *lis.* as they are scarce, so there is but little use of them yet, all Plantations being seated on the Rivers, they can go to and fro by Canoo or Boat as well and as soon as they can ride, the horses here like the Indians and many of the English do travail without shoes.   Now each family hath got a stock of Hogs and Cows, which when once a little more encreased, they may send of to the Islands cheaper then any other place can, by reason of its propinquity, which trade alone will make it far more considerable than either Virginia, Maryland, Pensilvania, and those other places to the North of us.

   I desire you would be pleased by the next opportunity to send me over the best herbalist for Physical Plants in as small a Volume as you can get.   There was a new one just came out as I left England, if I mistake not in 8ᵛᵒ. that was much commended, the Author I have forgot,[2] but there are severall in

Lords Proprietors pardoned him. See *Journal of the Grand Council of South Carolina*, 1671–1680 (Columbia, S. C., 1907), pp. 84–85. While hostilities were on with the Westoes the English furnished the Savannahs with arms with which to drive out their rivals, the Westoes, which they did in 1681.

   [1] See p. 158, *supra.*

   [2] Perhaps this was John Ray's *Methodus Plantarum Nova* (London, 1682, octavo).   If he received the "herbalist" it probably was included in the twenty-three books appraised in his inventory at £1. 10*s.*   See p. 179, *supra.*

the Colledge that can direct you to the best. If Mr. Sessions, Mr. Hobart or Mr. White, should send to you for money for the passage of a servant, whether man or boy that they Judge likely, I desire you would be pleased to send it them, for such will turn to good account here; and if you please to enquire at some Apothecarys what Sassafrass (which grows here in great plenty) is worth a pound and how and at what time of the year to cure it, let me know as soon as you can, for if the profit is not I am sure the knowledge is worth sending for. Pray Sir let me hear by the next how all our friends and relacions do, what change in the Colledge, and what considerable alteracion through the whole Town; I have now nothing more to speak but my desire that you may still retain (what I know you do) that love with which I dayly was blest and that readiness in pardoning whatsoever you find amiss, and to believe that my affections are not changed with the Climate unless like it too, grown warmer, this with my most humble duety to yourself and my mother, my kind love to my sister and Brothers and all the rest of our Friends I rest

Your most dutifull and obedient son,
THO: NEWE.

From Charls Town in Carolina.

From CHARLS TOWN, August the 23,
1682.

Most Honourd Father.

In obedience to your commands, I am ready to embrace every opportunity of sending to you, this is the 3rd, The 2 first by way of Barbados, the 1^{rst} of the 17th, the 2nd of the 29th of May, which I hope you will receive long before this comes to your hands. This place affords little news, nothing worth sending. The 11th of June a French Privateer of 4 Guns 30 men whereof 10 were English men brought in here a Spanish prize of 16 Guns and a 100 men, which by the Frenchmens confession they had never taken, had it not been for the English, they have allready spent most of it and are providing to be gone againe.

The 30th of July cam an Indian to our Governour and told him that 800 Spaniards were upon their march coming from St. Augustine (a place belonging to our Proprietors about 150

miles to the South of us, where the Spaniards are seated and
have a pretty strong Town) to fall upon the English, upon
which the Council met 3 times and ordered 20 great Guns
that lay at a place where the town was first designed to be
made, to be brought to Charls Town, and sent Scouts at a
good distance (knowing which way they must come) to discover
their strength and the truth of it, which if they had seen anything were to return with all speed, and 700 men were to have
met them, which were to lay in Ambuscade in a Cave, swam[1]
where the Spaniards were to come, through a Marsh, that
every step they would be up to their middle. Our people
were so far from being afraid that they mightily rejoyced at
the news of it, wishing that they might have some just cause
of War with the Spaniards, that they might grant Commissions to Privateers, and themselves fall on them at St. Augustine.[2] as we understand since this was the ground of the report,
The Spaniards thinking themselves to be abused by a nation
of Indians that lived betwixt them and us, marched out to
cut of that Nation, to which this Indian belonged, which (as
it is usual with the Indians) reported that they were 800,
whereas some of the Privateers have been there, and say that
they are not able to raise above 300 men. we have 100 Privateers here all shar like though not at the taking of the prize,
which if our Governour would suffer them would fain fall on
the Spaniards at St. Augustine; it is not likely if the Spaniards
were so strong as the Indian reported, that they would send
out such strength against them, For when the English have
any war with a Nation of the Indians tho at 150 miles distance they think 20 English and 30 or 40 friendly Indians to
be a sufficient party. The Indians are sent before to discover
where the other Indians lay who if they see but [gap in MS.]
of their enemyes they will returne with great speed and greater
fear to the English reporting they saw 200.
    The 20th of August I saw a Comet in the North East about
2 hours before day, the 21 it was seen in the west.[3] Sir of
those goods you gave me of my Brothers, I have sold some,

[1] Sic.
[2] "These sentiments were vividly manifested when the Spaniards actually
did attack, in 1686."—Jameson.
[3] Halley's comet was then visible.

and most of them I bought in London, but I can not yet make any returne; for money here is but little and that Spanish which will not go for so much in England by 4 or 5 s in the li. Our pay is what the Countrey affords, as Corn, Pork, Tar and Cedar, the 3 first are fit only for the Islands. I know not whether the last will pay charges to England it can't be afforded under 30 or 32 s profit in London, if you please you may enquire what it will yield in Oxon, and if you think it worth sending, and know how to dispose of it, I will take care to send it by the first, after I know your mind. Sir I have sent to Mr. Sessions for these following goods which are the best I can think of and I desire you, that you would let him have as much money as will buy them. Nuttmegs to the value of 5 li, Pepper 50 s, Cinnamon 25 s, Cloves and Mace 25 s, $\frac{1}{2}$ a C of large Beads, blue and white, or white with streaks of blue or black, or blew with beads blew and white, or white with streaks of blew or black, 1 [gap] of blew Duffals, a quarter of a Cask of brandy, $\frac{1}{2}$ doz white Castors, at about 8 or 10 s per piece, and one good French hat, 2 or 3 [gap] of fine thread to make lace, 500 small needles and 20 [gap] of that tape which is now in fashion to make lace with, 8 or 10 doz. of knives from 2 s 06 d to 5 s per doz., one good [gap] coat for myself and 2 C[1] of pigeon shot. Sir I desire you with these things to send me $\frac{1}{2}$ C of Shomakers thread and one of my Brothers shop books if you have one that is not used. Sir I beseech you pardon my presumption since 'twas your good ness made me so by your usuall readiness in granting my former requests. Pray present my humble duety to my Mother and my Grandmother, my kind love to my sister and Brothers and the rest of our Relations and be confident that I will be industrious to improve whatsoever you shall commit to my charge and to approve my self

Your most Dutifull and obedient Son,

THOMAS NEWE.

[1] *I. e.*, hundredweight.

CHARLESTON IN THE 1780'S

Johann David Schoepf visited the
United States during 1783 and 1784.
The following are his views of
Charleston.

Source: Alfred J. Morrison, trans. and ed. Travels
in the Confederation /1783-1784/, from the German
of Johann David Schoepf. Philadelphia: William
J. Campbell, 1911, vol. II, 164-170.

Charleston is one of the finest of American cities;
Philadelphia excepted, it is inferior to none, and I
know not whether, from its vastly more cheerful and
pleasing plan, it may not deserve first place, even if it
is not the equal of Philadelphia in size and population.
The city contains a number of tasteful and elegant
buildings, which however are mostly of timber. This
circumstance is explained in part by the natural
scarceness of stone in this region; but there seems no
reason why bricks might not be used here for building
quite as well as at Philadelphia and New York, since
nowhere are better materials to be had, or in greater
plenty. The number of the houses is estimated to be
about 1500. In the plan of the houses especial regard
is had to airy and cool rooms. Most of the houses
have spacious yards and gardens, and the kitchen is
always placed in a separate building, the custom
throughout the southern provinces, to avoid the heat
and the danger of fire. The chief streets are wide,
straight, and cross at right angles; but they are not
paved, and hence give rise to a double inconvenience,
in rainy and in dusty weather. The greatest length of
the city is little short of a mile.

Its situation is 32° 40′ n. latitude, and 83° 40′ w.
longitude, on a point of land between the Cowper and
the Ashley rivers, the spot where Captain Sayle landed
the first planters in the year 1669, settling there with

them because, for fear of the savages, they dared not strike farther inland. A plan for the building of a magnificent city was sketched and sent over by the Lords Proprietors, to whom King Charles the Second had assigned the province of Carolina, but so far this has not been fully carried out.

Both the rivers named are navigable, but for trading-vessels only the Cowper as much as 20 miles above the city. Merchant-men find commodious and safe anchorage between the city and a little island in the Cowper river. This part of the river is called the Bay, and along this side of the city the shore is furnished with excellent wharves of cabbage-trees. The entrance to the harbor is made more difficult by a bar which ships of more than 200 tons cannot pass without lightening cargo. The advantageous site of the city has not been neglected in its fortification; towards the land side as well as at the south-western point there have long been regular works of masonry, which during the war were considerably increased and improved both by the Americans and the English, but are now again fallen to decay. On the landside the city has but one approach, protected by a gate with several walled defences of oyster-shells and lime. Among the public buildings of the city the handsome State-house, the Main-guard opposite, the Bourse, and the two churches, St. Philipp and St. Michael, are conspicuous, all designed after good plans. Two lines of framed barracks, for the one-time English garrisons are not at present made use of. The tower of St. Michael's church is 190 feet high, and has long served as landmark for incoming ships. It was formerly painted white; the American Commodore Whipple hit upon the idea of painting it black on the side towards the sea whence it can be seen very far, so as to make it invisible to British ships, whose visits were dreaded. But the result so far from being that desired was directly the opposite, for in clear weather the black side is far more distinct, and on gloomy, cloudy days it is seen quite as far and appears, if anything, larger than before.

There is a German Lutheran congregation here, with its own church and minister, but it it not very numerous.

The name of the city, since the last peace, has been changed from Charlestown to Charleston, and at the same time its rank, that of a Town until then, made that of a City. By the English rule those towns only are called cities which have a Bishop and are incor-

porated, or those which exercise their own granted
privileges under the presidency of a Mayor and other
officers and use a special city-seal. A bishop Charleston has not, but the dignity of a Mayor, called Super-
intendent, has been given it under this elevation of
rank conferred by the Provincial Assembly.

The number of the inhabitants was formerly reck-
oned at 10-12000, of which half or probably two thirds
were blacks, but at present it is not possible to say
exactly what the number is, since no precise baptismal
or death lists are kept. The population, besides, has
considerably diminished both by voluntary emigration
and by the banishment of many of the most estimable
citizens of the royalist party. But certainly the number of the white inhabitants is greatly less than that
of the blacks, browns, and yellows to be seen here of
all shades. In winter the city is less active than in
summer. About Christmas most of the families re-
tire to their country-seats, and spend there the greater
part of what remains of the winter. One reason for this
is that at that festival season the negroes are allowed
somewhat more liberty, and fearing they might use it
in a bad way, the proprietors deem it well to be present themselves and at the same time look after the
progress of their plantation affairs. With the coming
of the sweltry summer days all that can hasten back
to town. The nearness of the sea and the cooler winds
blowing thence make summer in the city pleasanter
and wholesomer than farther inland among woods and
swamps.

The manners of the inhabitants of Charleston are as
different from those of the other North American
cities as are the products of their soil. The profitable
rice and indigo plantations are abundant sources of
wealth for many considerable families, who therefore
give themselves to the enjoyment of every pleasure
and convenience to which their warmer climate and
better circumstances invite them. Throughout, there
prevails here a finer manner of life, and on the whole
there are more evidences of courtesy than in the northern cities. I had already been told this at Philadelphia, and I found it to be the case; just as in general on the way hither, the farther I travelled from
Pensylvania towards the southern country, there were
to be observed somewhat more pleasing manners
among the people, at least there was absent the un-
bearable curiosity of the common sort, which in the
more northern regions extends to shamelessness and
exhausts all patience. There is courtesy here, without punctiliousness, stiffness, or formality. It has

long been nothing extraordinary for the richer inhabitants to send their children of both sexes to
Europe for their education. The effect of this on
manners must be all the greater and more general
since there were neither domestic circumstances to
stand in the way nor particular religious principles, as
among the Presbyterians of New England or the
Quakers of Pensylvania, to check the enjoyment of
good-living. So luxury in Carolina has made the
greatest advance, and their manner of life, dress,
equipages, furniture, everything denotes a higher degree of taste and love of show, and less frugality than
in the northern provinces. They had their own play-
house, in which itinerant companies from time to time
entertained the public, but it was burned some time
ago. A like misfortune overtook an elegant dancing-
hall. A French dancing master was the promoter of
this building; the necessary amount was advanced him
by the first minister of the town who not only had no
hesitation in a matter of furthering the pleasure of his
parishioners, but afterwards when the property fell to
him, the Frenchman being unable to return the loan,
made no scruple of receiving the rent; whereas in the
New England states the bare thought of such a thing
would have disgraced any minister. Pleasures of
every kind are known, loved, and enjoyed here.
There are publick concerts, at this time mainly under
the direction of German and English musicians left
behind by the army, for as yet few of the natives care
greatly for music or understand it. A liking for exclusive private societies, Clubs so-called, prevails here
very generally. There are as many as 20 different
Clubs, and most of the residents are members of more
than one. These social unions give themselves strange
names at times, as: Mount Sion Society, Hell-fire
Club, Marine Anti-Britannic Society, Smoaking Society, and the like. All the games usual in England
are in vogue here. As regards dress, the English
taste is closely followed; also the clergy and civil
officers wear the garb customary in England. The
ladies bestow much attention upon their dress, and
spare no cost to obtain the newest modes from Europe.
Milliners and hair-dressers do well here and grow
rich.

Charleston, at sundry times and by opposite ele-
ments, has been threatened with complete destruction.
A great part of the town has several times gone up in
fire, and with a loss of considerable stores of mer-
chants' wares. Again, violent and lasting hurricanes

have seemed as if certain to destroy the place. The low situation of the town exposes it, if north-east storms hold somewhat long, to the danger of furious overflow, these winds checking the northwestern course of the gulf-stream flowing along the coast from the Mexican gulf, and driving it and other water of the ocean against the flat coast of Carolina. From the same causes also the two rivers flowing by the town are checked, and in a very brief space the water often rises to an incredible height.

In the item of weather Carolina is subject to the same changes as the rest of the eastern coast of North America; warmth and cold, fair and rainy days are the effects or consequences of the winds. The North-west spreads cold over this southern region as over all the coast besides. In January and February 1784, the time of my stay at Charleston, the weather was almost regularly cyclical, as follows: North-east winds brought cloudy weather and rain—until, commonly, the wind changed of a sudden to north-west, and there was clear, dry weather; if the wind held in this quarter or blew strong, there was more or less cold.* The north-wester is generally followed by milder winds from the West, which gradually work more around to the South, until finally the winds are hardly perceptible from the South, or there is calm, during which time the weather is fine and warm as a rule, until the wind rises again from the east or the north-east, the weather changing in a similar way. This same succession of winds and weather holds pretty well throughout eastern North America, if there is no disturbance from extraordinary causes. The north-east winds always rise first in those parts most to the south, and show their effects later and later in the more northern provinces. One may convince himself of this by following every account given in the publick prints of violent storms from that quarter and the damage done shipping along the entire coast; it will be found that a north-east storm is remarked earliest in Carolina or Virginia, then in Pensylvania, next in New York, and often a day later, or even more, in New England. ✛

---

* " For Carolina and Florida higher mountains would be of " advantage and a protection against the cold north-west " winds." Molina, *Storia naturale del Chili.*—For more regarding the state of the air, winds, and climate of South Carolina, Vid. Chalmers, *Account[F] of the weather & diseases of S. Carolina;* Preface.

SOUTH CAROLINA IN THE 1820'S

The following is a detailed
description of Charleston
economic and social life as
well as the conditions of
slavery during the 1820's.

Source: Captain Basil Hall. Travels in North America
In the Years 1827 and 1828. Edinburgh: Printed for
Cadell and Co., and Simplein and Marshall, London,
1829, vol. II, 139-170.

' Charleston is a very pretty-looking city, stand-
ing on a dead level, with the sea in front, and two
noble rivers, the Ashley and the Cooper, enclosing
it on a wide peninsula called the Neck. This space
of flat ground is covered with the villas of the
wealthy planters, many of which were almost hid
in the rich foliage, which even at this early season
was in great beauty.   In the streets, a row of trees
is planted on each side, along the outer edge of the
foot pavement, a fashion common to most of the
southern towns of America. This tree is generally
called the Pride of India, the botanical name being,
I believe, Melia Azedarach. From the top of the
trunk, which is cut off or pollarded, a number of
long slender arms shoot out, bearing bunches of
leaves at the extremity. The spring was not far
advanced, but most of these trees were budding,
and some were in leaf. 'What gives Charleston its
peculiar character, however, is the verandah, or.

piazza, which embraces most of the houses on their
southern side, and frequently, also, on those which
face the east and west. These are not clumsily put
on, but constructed in a light Oriental style, extend-
ing from the ground to the very top, so that the
rooms on each story enjoy the advantage of a shady,
open walk. Except in the busy, commercial parts
of the town, where building ground is too precious
to be so employed, the houses are surrounded by a
garden, crowded with shrubs and flowers of all
kinds, shaded by double and treble rows of orange
trees ; each establishment being generally encircled
by hedges of a deep green, covered over with the
most brilliant show imaginable of large white roses,
fully as broad as my hand.

, The houses, which stand in the midst of these
luxurious pleasure grounds, are built of every form
and size, generally painted white, with railed ter-
races on the tops, and every house, or very nearly
every one, and certainly every church spire, of
which there are a great number, has a lightning
rod, or conductor, in the efficacy of which, by the
way, the inhabitants of America have more faith
than I think we have in Europe.

I was much struck with the sort of tropical as-
pect which belonged more to the port of Charleston than to any other I saw in America. I remember one day in particular, when, tempted by
the hopes of catching a little of the cool sea breeze,
I strolled to the shore. In two minutes after leaving the principal street, I found myself alongside
of vessels from all parts of the world, loading and
unloading their cargoes. On the wharf, abreast
of a vessel just come in from the Havannah, I observed a great pile of unripe bananas, plucked from
the trees only four or five days before in the Island
of Cuba. Close by these stood a pyramid of cocoa
nuts, equally fresh, some with their husks still on,
some recently stripped of their tough wiry coating.
The seamen were hoisting out of the hold of a ship,
bags of coffee and large oblong boxes of sugar ;
while a little further up the quay, two negro coopers

—whose broken English and peculiar Creole tone
showed them to be natives of some French West
India Island—were busily employed heading up
casks of rice to be shipped in this vessel, as soon
as the productions of a still warmer climate should
be removed from her.

On every side, the ground was covered, in true
commercial style, with great bales of cotton, boxes
of fruit, barrels of flour, and large square cases
of goods, built one upon the top of another, with
the owner's initials painted upon them, within
mystical circles and diamonds, visible between
the crossings of the cords which had held them
tight on their voyage from Europe or from India.

The whole scene, though any thing but new to
me, was certainly not on that account less pleasing.
The day, also, was bright and sunny, and the numerous vessels which fringed the wharf, or were
scattered over the ample bay, were lying with their
sails loosed to dry. I almost fancied myself again
in the equatorial regions; a vision which brought
many scenes of past voyages crowding upon my
recollection. I thought of Java—Bermuda—St
Christopher's, and the most beautiful of all, Ceylon.
Every object on which the eye rested, was in character with those countries, from the dripping fore-
head of the poor negro, to the cotton sails of the
schooners, the luxuriant fruits of the Caribee
Islands, and the blue heavens of a perpetual summer. I felt myself hurried back to seas and lands
which, if revisited, might not, perhaps, be enjoyed as they once were, but which I shall certainly
never forget, as having, in their brilliant reality,
far exceeded the wildest conceptions which imagination had ventured to paint of those fairy regions
—by some people supposed to have no existence
but in the vivid colouring of the poet. Alas! how
tame the liveliest creations of fancy appear, when
placed by the side even of a limited experience!

But, after all, the most picturesque object in
every traveller's landscape is generally the Post-
office; and drawing myself away from these de-

licious scenes, some real and some imaginary, I
set off in quest of letters. My attention, however,
was arrested on the way by a circumstance which
I might certainly have expected in Charleston, but
somehow had not looked for. On reaching the Exchange, in the centre of which the Post-office is
placed, I heard the sound of several voices in the
street, like those of an auctioneer urging an audi-
ence to bid for his goods. I walked to the side of
the gallery overlooking a court or square, in which
a number of people were collected to purchase
slaves and other property. One man was selling
a horse on which he was mounted, and riding up
and down the streets; another, in the same way,
was driving about in a curricle, bawling out to
the spectators to make an offer for his carriage
and horses. But of course my attention was most
taken up with the slave market.

A long table was placed in the middle of the
street, upon which the negroes were exposed, not
one by one, but in families at a time. From this
conspicuous station they were shown off by two
auctioneers, one at each end of the table, who
called out the biddings, and egged on the pur-
chasers by chanting the praises of their bargains.

These parties of slaves varied in number. The
first consisted of an old, infirm woman, a stout
broad-shouldered man, apparently her son, his
wife, and two children. The auctioneer, having
told the names of each, and described their qualifications, requested the surrounding gentlemen
to bid. One hundred dollars for each member of
the family, or 500 for the whole party, was the
first offer. This gradually rose to 150, at which
sum they were finally knocked down; that is to
say, 750 dollars for the whole, or about L.170.
Several other families were then put up in succession, who brought from 250 to 260 dollars each
member, including children at the breast, as well
as old people quite incapable of work.

The next party was exceedingly interesting.
The principal person was a stout well-built man,

or, as the auctioneer called him, " a fellow, who was a capital driver." His wife stood by his side— a tall, finely proportioned, and really handsome woman, though as black as jet. Her left arm encircled a child about six months old, who rested, in the Oriental fashion, on the hip bone. To preserve the balance, her body was inclined to the right, where two little urchins clung to her knee, one of whom, evidently much frightened, clasped its mother's hand, and never relinquished it during the sale which followed. The husband looked grave and somewhat sad; but there was a manliness in the expression of his countenance, which appeared strange in a person p.aced in so degraded a situation. What struck me most, however, was an occasional touch of anxiety about his eye as it glanced from bidder to bidder, when new offers were made. It seemed to imply a perfect acquaintance with the character of the different parties competing for him—and his happiness or misery for life, he might think, turned upon a word!

. The whole of this pretty group were neatly dressed, and altogether so decorous in their manner, that I felt my interest in them rising at every instant. The two little boys, who appeared to be twins, kept their eyes fixed steadily on their mother's face. At first they were quite terrified, but eventually they became as tranquil as their parents. The struggle amongst the buyers continued for nearly a quarter of an hour, till at length they were knocked down for 290 dollars a-piece, or 1450 dollars for the whole family, about L.330 Sterling.

I learnt from a gentleman afterwards that the negroes, independently of the important consideration of being purchased by good masters, have a singular species of pride on these occasions in fetching a high price; holding it, amongst themselves, as disgraceful to be sold for a small sum of money. This fact, besides showing how difficult it is to subdue utterly the love of distinction, may perhaps be useful in teaching us never to take for granted that any one boasting the human form, however degraded in the scale, is without some traces of generous feeling. Indeed, I have frequently heard from judicious and kind-hearted slave-holders—for many such there are in America—that however difficult and thankless it often proves, yet there is always sufficient encouragement—sometimes as a matter of feeling, sometimes as a matter of interest—to treat these poor people not as the inferior animals, with so many of whose attributes we are apt to invest them, but, on the contrary, as men gifted more or less with generous motives capable of being turned to account.

At noon, accompanied by one of the most attentive and useful of the numerous friends we had the pleasure to make in America, we drove to the race ground, where we had the satisfaction of seeing a sharply contested match.

There was no great show of carriages, and not above a dozen ladies on the stand, although the day was fine enough to have tempted all the world abroad. I was informed by at least twenty different persons, that this was a most unfavourable specimen of the races, which of late years had been falling off, chiefly, it has been suggested, in consequence of the division of property, by which so many of the large estates had been melted down. Those great landed proprietors, who in all countries are the true supporters of these expensive but useful amusements, and who used in former days to give such eclat to the Charleston races, are no longer to be found on the turf.

During the interval between the heats, one of those rows, which appear to belong, as a matter of course, to such a place, occurred in front of the stand. Some squabble arose between a tall farmer-looking man, and a sailor. Words of great bitterness were hastily followed by blows, upon which the parties had their coats off in a twinkling. I watched with much curiosity to see how such matters were settled in America, where prize-fighting is not more in fashion than it is in Scotland. In

merry England, ' a ring! a ring!' would have
been vociferated by a hundred mouths—seconds
would have stepped forward—fair play would have
been insisted upon—and the whole affair finally
adjusted in four or five minutes. One or other of
the combatants might have got a sound drubbing,
and both would certainly have been improved in
manners, for the remainder of that day at least.

It was quite differently settled, however, on this
occasion. Several persons rushed out of the crowd,
and instead of making them fight it out manfully,
separated the disputants by force, who, nevertheless, continued abusing one another outrageously.
Not content with this, each of the high contending
parties, having collected a circle of auditors round
him, delivered a course of lectures on the merits
of the quarrel, till, instead of a single pair of brawl-
ers, there were at least a dozen couples, inter-
changing oaths and scurrility in the highest style
of seaport eloquence.

Where this tumult would have ended, if there
had been no interference, it is difficult to guess;
but presently a man came with a whip in his hand,
with which he very soon cleared the course. This
was quite necessary, indeed, as the horses were
ready to start; but he carried his operations further than I had any idea would have been permitted. He cut at the men as well as the boys, not
in jest, but with some severity. How all this came
to be submitted to, in this land of the free, I could
not find out. One gentleman to whom I applied
for a solution of this mystery, said the offenders
were well served, as they had no business to be in
the way. Another went so far as to use the facts
I have just stated, to illustrate the love of good
order, and the ready obedience which the Ameri-
çans yield to lawful authority. I should just like,
however, to see a similar experiment tried at Ep-
som or Doncaster! There would soon be a fine row,
and if the whip and the whipper did not speedily
vanish over the ropes, I am much mistaken. -

On the evening of the 29th of February, we attended a ball given in the great rooms belonging to the St Andrews Society, to which we had been most kindly invited by the Jockey Club of Charleston.

A traveller should speak with great caution—I may say reluctance—of the private manners and customs of foreign countries, since there is almost a universal unwillingness amongst the natives to be commented upon, in these respects, even when nothing is found fault with. Nevertheless, so many characteristic features of every country are displayed in ball-rooms or other public assemblies, that where no personal descriptions are thought of, or can by any means be made applicable, it may be allowable occasionally to advert to such things for the purpose of illustrating graver matters. If such inferences be drawn with fairness and good-humour, the natives themselves ought, I think, to be rather amused than otherwise, by seeing themselves reflected from the mirror of a stranger's mind. At all events, I am sure, for my own part, I have laughed heartily at the graphic accounts I have read of Edinburgh parties, in more than one American book of travels.

The room was large, the ball handsomely got up, and every thing ordered in the best style, with one small exception—the ladies and gentlemen appeared to be entire strangers to one another. The ladies were planted firmly along the walls, in the coldest possible formality, while the gentlemen, who, except during the dance, stood in close column near the door, seemed to have no fellow-feeling, nor any wish to associate with the opposite sex.

In the ordinary business of their lives—I mean their busy, money-making, electioneering lives—the Americans have little or no time for companionship, that I could ever see or hear of, with the women, still less for any habitual confidential intercourse. Consequently, when they come together for the express purpose of amusement, those easy and familiar habits which are essential to the cheerfulness of a ball-room, or indeed of any room, are rarely to be found.

In place of that unreserved but innocent freedom of manners, which forms one of the highest charms of polished society elsewhere, I must say that I seldom observed any thing in America but the most respectful and icy propriety upon all occasions when young people of different sexes were brought together. Positively I never once, during the whole period I was in that country, saw any thing approaching, within many degrees, to what we should call a Flirtation; I mean that sedulous and exclusive attention paid to one person above all others, and which may by that person not be unkindly received. Without being called attachment, it often borders so closely upon it, that mere proximity and frequency of intercourse, tend to sustain a lambent fire beneath, which may be fanned into flame, or be allowed to expire, according as circumstances, upon further acquaintance, prove suitable or otherwise. This degree of incipient interest, sometimes felt by one, sometimes shared by both, will often admit of ample expression, not only without evil consequences to the young parties themselves, but with eminent advantage both to them, and to society. For nothing but good can possibly spring out of a well-regulated exercise of some of the purest and most generous feelings of our nature. I suspect, however, that it is quite essential to the attainment of any high degree of refinement in society, that the practice of expressing such emotions, and many others of a similar character, should be habitual, and not contingent.

Such a degree of freedom of manners cannot, I fear, exist in a society like that of America, where, from its very nature, the rules of behaviour cannot yet have become settled. The absence of all classification of ranks, prevents people from becoming sufficiently well acquainted with one another to justify such intimacies. Or, it may be that in places where an artificial system of manners, appropriate to each class respectively, has not been adopted by general consent, to regulate the intercourse alluded to, there might be some difficulty in keeping matters within due limits.

In older countries, from long and universal usage —from whose laws no one ever dreams of departing—people go on from year to year with such perfect confidence in one another, that many things are not only looked upon as perfectly innocent and proper, but, from mere habit, become almost integral parts of the system of manners, although in so young a country as America, where nothing of the kind has the sanction of custom, they would probably be considered highly indecorous.

It would be unreasonable to find fault with these characteristic attributes of American manners, and nothing certainly is further from my intention, than any such censure. My wonder, on the contrary is, how a society, such as we actually see there, has sprung up in a country where the property is so equally divided,—where consequently there can be no permanent distinctions of wealth and rank, and the great body of the people are employed nearly in the same pursuit, while such numerous and exciting distractions occur to unsettle all men's thoughts and habits—most of them tending rather to prevent than to encourage the growth of the refinements of life.

To return to very different matters, I may mention, that there are few things against which a traveller in search of information has so much occasion to guard himself, as the very natural prejudices of the people living on the spot. Residents seldom, if ever, imagine it possible that they can be under the influence of those mistaken feelings, which they ascribe so freely to their guests. The reason is obvious. They possess so great a store of facts, they fancy they cannot possibly err—while the stranger, who is acquainted with only a small portion of these, must, in their opinion, inevitably go wrong. But I should like to know what the poor stranger is to do when he meets equally well-informed natives, who take diametrically opposite views of the very same question? In this dilemma

lies the danger; for it is always more gratifying
to our self-love, and more convenient in every
way, to consider that man right whose opinions
coincide with our own, than to exchange views with
one who thinks differently from us. Nothing is
more easy in the practice of travelling, as I have
often experienced, than to find supporters on the
spot to the most extravagant of our fancies; and,
I presume, it is on this account that the natives
of every country will bear with more patience the
genuine strictures of a foreigner, than they will
listen to the criticisms which, if so disposed, he
may always cull from amongst themselves, in order
to quote against them.

For example, if it were my wish—which it is
not—to represent the Americans as generally in-
different to the evils of slavery, I could easily support my opinion by bringing forward the insulated
authority of persons, whose names would carry
with them considerable weight, and who, I believe,
are so sincere, that I do not imagine they would
object to my mentioning whence I derived my information. Yet the impression conveyed by their
opinions would, nevertheless, be far from correct,
as applied generally to the inhabitants of that country.

" For my part," said one of these gentlemen to
me, " I consider slavery as no evil at all. On the
contrary, I think it a great good; and, upon the
whole, I look upon it as a wise arrangement, quite
as consistent with the ordering of Providence as
any thing else we see."

" You surprise me exceedingly," I replied. " I
wish you would tell me on what grounds you maintain so singular a doctrine."

" It is obvious," he continued, " that there must
be hewers of wood and drawers of water in the
world—you grant me that?"

" Oh! freely."

" Well, then, I contend, that by the slave system, these necessary labours—irksome and disagreeable in themselves, but still indispensable—

are actually performed at a smaller expense of
human suffering by slaves, than by any other system that has yet been devised. That is to say, the
same work is executed here in the slave-holding
States, with less unhappiness than in our northern
non-slave-holding States ; and with still less misery
than in England, where all the property is in the
hands of one-tenth part of the population, and the
other nine-tenths are in a state of starvation, and
consequently, of discontent, and of hostility to
their task-masters."

" And what sort of happiness," I asked, " have
these slaves, whom you place above your free coun-
trymen ?"

" They work much less," he said, " they are as
well fed—they have no care for the future—very
little for the present—they are in a state of happy
ignorance, and know nothing of those things which
make freemen miserable ; and as they are generally well used, they become attached to their masters,
and work on in their service cheerfully."

" Yes," I said, " but have they a single generous
motive to incite them to labour ? Can they choose
their own master ? Are they not sold and bought,
and separated from one another like cattle ? And,
in spite of all the degradation you can heap upon
them, have they not a distinct perception that the
Whites are better off than they can ever be ?

" In the mean time, it is in vain to deny that—
circumstanced as they now are—the negroes belong almost to a different race—so different, that
no philanthropist or abolitionist, however enthu-
siastic, pretends to say that an amalgamation can
take place between them and the whites. There
is no reasoning upon this point—it seems a law of
our nature, and is felt, probably, as strongly in
other countries as here. What English gentleman,
for example, would give his daughter in marriage
to a negro ? But the prejudice, or whatever it be,

is just as strong in the Southern States of America, with respect to a political community of rights and privileges. And if changes in this respect are ever to be brought about, they can only be accomplished by the slowest conceivable degrees. In the State of New York, the negroes have the privilege of voting; and you will see over the country many mulattoes : but these are mere drops in the ocean of this dark question; and we are still centuries before that period which many very sincere men believe has already arrived.

" No one can tell how these things will modify themselves in time. There may be many bloody insurrections, aided by foreign enemies—or the States may separate, and civil wars ensue—or servile wars may follow—or the blacks and whites may, in process of ages, by the combination of some moral and political miracle, learn to assimilate; but, in the mean time, I suspect the present generation can do nothing of any consequence to advance such an object. The blacks, who form our labouring population, are so deplorably ignorant, and so vicious, that in almost every instance where freedom has been given to them, they have shown how unfit they are to make a right use of it. The practice of manumission is, in consequence, every where discouraged, and in many places rendered by law impossible, except in cases of high public service."

Slavery, then, according to this gentleman, so far from being a benefit, is a very great evil in every sense of the word. All practical men, he assured me, admitted that the amount of work done by the slaves, generally speaking, is the very lowest possible, and of the worst quality ; for since the fear of the lash is their chief motive to exertion, so every art which ingenuity, uncontrolled by any considerations of truth, can devise, is put in force to evade their assigned tasks.

In talking of emancipation, people are apt to forget various little difficulties which stand in the way. In the first place, the slaves are, to all intents and purposes, the property of the whites. They have been legally acquired, they are held legally, and the produce of their labour forms the rightful fortune of their masters. To enter the warehouses of the Planters, and rob them of their rice or cotton, would not be one whit more unjust than taking away the slaves whose labour brings it out of the ground. Suppose, however, that difficulty removed, and that a compensation could be provided for the slaveholder, what is to become of the liberated negroes? What is to be done with two millions of ignorant persons, brought up, as their fathers and ancestors were, in bodily and mental bondage,—who have acquired habits of thinking and feeling suitable to that state, but totally unfit for any other? It is said to be less difficult to make a slave of a freeman, than to raise a slave to a just knowledge of freedom. And certainly experience in America gives no reason to hope that this maxim is there reversed. The mere act of breaking the chains will not do. The rivets that have so long held down the understanding cannot be driven out, till some contrivance be found which shall at the same time eradicate all memory of the past, and all associations with the present state of the world, from the minds not of the blacks alone, but also of the whites. If we examine this matter closely, we shall find the difficulty increased by discovering, that a slave is, strictly speaking, a pauper both in his person and his intellects; for while he is fed and clothed by others, he is likewise supplied with thoughts and motives to action—such as they are!—not from the spontaneous or regulated impulse of his own faculties, but by the superior—I may say exclusive, will of his master. This is no exaggeration. It has always been so, and must long remain thus.

How is it possible, then, if all these things be taken into consideration, to suppose that people so very differently circumstanced can be admitted at once to the common privileges of freedom? Or, how, on the other hand, can it be expected that the masters of these slaves, who, like their fathers before them, have derived their whole substance from this source,—who look to it as a provision for their descendants,—and who know that their title is strictly a legal one, can be willing to allow of such interference as shall have a direct tendency to withdraw from them the whole sum and substance of their fortunes?

Some people may suppose I am fighting with men of straw, set up only to be knocked down, and that notions so unreasonable as these cannot enter seriously into any man's mind. But the contrary is too generally the case, and was at one time, indeed, my own view of the matter. At all events, be this as it may, the Southern planters, who have the power completely in their hands, seem resolved to maintain the present system; and I am quite sure they will maintain it inviolate, in spite of their own admission that it is a grievous evil, and certainly in spite of all attempts to compel them to change it.

This melancholy prospect, nevertheless, is not altogether without a gleam of hope, as I had the satisfaction of discovering when I pushed my enquiries further. By gradually acquiring a more extensive knowledge of the facts of the case under many different forms, I was enabled, I trust, to escape from the influence of enthusiasm or of paradox on the one hand, and of strong, and often angry passions and interests on the other. To steer a fair course in the midst of such a strange kind of moral and political navigation is a hard task for any traveller, and doubly so for one to whom the subject is entirely new.

On the 4th of March we performed a round of sight-seeing at Charleston, by visiting in the course of the morning the Orphan Asylum, the Work House, the Poor House, the Jail, besides examining an extensive rice mill. It is not possible to describe all these institutions with the minuteness which their importance would seem to require; and, indeed, my object in visiting them was more to gain a general acquaintance with the habits

of the people amongst whom I was mixing, and
their ways of thinking, than to investigate closely the particular objects which they were always
ready most kindly to bring under my notice.
When men are mounted on their own favourite
hobbies, they are far more apt to let themselves out,
as it is called, and to betray the real state of their
thoughts and feelings, than at any other moment,
when perhaps they may be on their guard. I do
not mean that I had any desire to watch or spy out
things which people wished to conceal ;—quite the
contrary. I merely tried to get hold of them at
those moments when their habitual reserve was
merged so completely in the interest of their own
especial topics, that they themselves were anxious
to communicate the information required, exactly
as it stood, uncoloured by any studied descriptions,
got up with a view to the honour and glory of the
nation—a vice to which the people of all countries are more or less prone in speaking to a
stranger.

Our first visit was to a Rice Mill, where I learnt
that the grains of this plant grow on separate pedicles, or little fruit stalks, springing from the main
stalk. The whole head forms what a botanist would
call a spiked panicle ; that is, something between
a spike like wheat, and a panicle like oats. From
these pedicles the rice must be separated by the
hand-flail, as no machinery has yet been devised
for effecting this purpose. The next process is to
detach the outer husk, which clings to the grain
with great pertinacity. This is done by passing
the rice between a pair of mill-stones, removed
to a considerable distance from each other. The
inner pellicle, or film, which envelopes the grain,
is removed by trituration in mortars under pestles weighing from 250 to 200 pounds. These
pestles consist of upright bars, shod with iron,
which being raised up by the machinery to the
height of several feet, are allowed to fall plump
down upon the rice, the particles of which are
thus rubbed against one another till the film is

removed. It is now thoroughly winnowed, and
being packed in casks holding about 600 pounds
each, is ready for distribution over all parts of the
world.

Rice with the husk on, or what is technically
called Paddy—a word borrowed from India—will
keep fresh and good for a much longer time than
after it has undergone the two processes above described. Besides which, prepared rice is apt to
become dusty, either from exposure or from rub-
bing about in the carriage, on board ship, and in
the warehouses on both sides of the Atlantic. These
facts recently suggested to some enterprising ca-
pitalists to bring it to England in the shape of
paddy, and there to detach the husk. This experiment has been completely successful, as I can
testify from my own ample experience; for I have
frequently, since my return, eaten rice managed in
this way by Messrs Lucas and Ewbank of London, as fresh in taste and in appearance as any
I met with in South Carolina.

The Orphan Asylum of Charleston, like all
such institutions when well managed, is a most
interesting sight, however questionable the policy
may be, which, by holding out artificial means
of subsistence to families, gives a hurtful degree
of stimulus to the increase of population, already
but too apt to run into excess. It may seem ab-
surd to talk of over-population in America, but
I found at every one of the great towns on their
'sea board,' the evil of redundancy in this respect
grievously complained of. In the back woods, it
is a different affair; but the temptations to remain
amidst the comparative luxuries of the coast are
so great, that pauperism and destitution of various
kinds are fast becoming heavy loads upon the public
purse of all the States bordering on the Atlantic.

While looking at this Orphan Asylum, my attention was called to some curious features of
American society, which contradistinguish it from
that of old countries. All the world in that
busy land is more or less on the move, and as the

whole community is made up of units, amongst
which there is little of the principle of cohesion,
they are perpetually dropping out of one another's
sight, in the wide field over which they are scattered. Even the connexions of the same family
are soon lost sight of—the children glide away from
their parents, long before their manhood ripens;—
brothers and sisters stream off to the right and left,
mutually forgetting one another, and being forgot-
ten by their families. Thus, it often happens, that
the heads of a household die off, or wander away,
no one knows where, and leave children, if not
quite destitute, at least dependent on persons whose
connexion and interest in them are so small, that
the public eventually is obliged to take care of them,
from the impossibility of discovering any one whose
duty it is to give them a home. At Charleston,
Savannah, and other parts of the country where
the yellow fever occurs frequently, and where that
still more dreadful curse of America—spirit-drink-
ing—prevails, to at least as great an excess as in
the other States, it very often happens that children are left, at the end of the sickly season, without any relations, or natural protectors at all. Of
course, I speak now of the poorer inhabitants, part
of whom are made up of emigrants, either from
foreign countries, or from other parts of America.
It seems, indeed, to be the propensity of needy
persons in all countries to flock to great cities,
where they generally aggravate in a great degree
their own evils and those of the city.

The wealthier inhabitants of these towns, though
they cannot interfere to prevent such things, are
universally ready, not only with their money, but
with their personal exertions, to relieve the dis-
tress of their less fortunate fellow creatures; and
I must say, for the honour of the Americans, that
nothing can be more energetic than the way in
which they set about the establishment and main-
tenance of their public charities. Some of these
institutions may possibly be questionable in their
good effects on society, but there is never any de-

ficiency of zeal or liberality in their support.

The Workhouse, which we next visited, is a sort of Bridewell, where several parties of offenders were at work on the tread-wheel—the only one which I saw in action in America, and with no great effect, I was told. It seems, indeed, an essential part of the system of slavery, that the lash should be used as a means of enforcing obedience. But as the disagreeable nature of this discipline prevents the master from administering it at home, the offending slave is sent to the Workhouse with a note and a piece of money, on delivering which he receives so many stripes, and is sent back again.

In a free country, it may be useful to remember, the whole population enjoy the common protection of the laws; every one being subjected, if he offend, to the same penalties. But in a slaveholding country, an immense mass of people—the entire labouring class—are deprived of the advantages of the law, while they are exempted from none of its rigours. In a free country, accordingly, the laws are the supreme authority;—but in such a country as I am now alluding to, this authority, as far as the Blacks are concerned, is usurped, or, at all events, is virtually delegated by the laws to the masters, who, in most cases, are obliged to act as judge, jury, and executioner. From their decision the slave has no appeal, except in cases of rare enormity. Thus the masters, in point of fact, possess almost the exclusive administration of the laws, as far as concerns their slaves.

This arrangement, though it be most painful to think upon, and ten times more painful to witness, was described to me, and I much fear with justice, as being absolutely indispensable to the permanence of the system. At least I was often assured by sensible men, that any considerable modification of it, in principle or in practice, would speedily bring about anarchy, insurrection, bloodshed, and all the horrors of a servile war.

It would have required a much longer residence on the spot than I could afford, with many addi-

tional sources of information, which I did not possess, to have enabled me to say how far this stern
discipline was necessary to the peace of the country. In the meantime it does exist in the manner
I state, to the fullest extent, and I leave it to the
candour of any rational American to say, whether,
in the whole range of paradox, there is to be found
a greater absurdity than the attempt to set up a
population so governed, as at all comparable to that
of a country like Great Britain.

In the jail there were no separate sleeping births
for the prisoners, who appeared to pass their days
and nights in idleness and free communication.
At one part of the prison I saw several small cells
for different descriptions of convicts, who, however, had no labour to perform. The jailor told
me, that though he never put more than one white
man into these places, the blacks came so thick
upon him, he was often obliged to put in two at
a time.

In the court-yard of the jail, there were scattered about no fewer than 300 slaves, mostly brought
from the country for sale, and kept there at 20
cents, or about tenpence a-day, penned up like
cattle, till the next market day. The scene was
not unlike what I suppose the encampment of a
wild African horde to be—such as I have heard
Major Denham describe. Men, women, and children, of all ages, were crowded together in groups,
or seated in circles, round fires, cooking their
messes of Indian corn or rice. Clothes of all co-
lours were hung up to dry on the wall of the prison, coarse and ragged, while the naked children
were playing about quite merrily, unconscious,
poor little wretches! alike of their present degradation, and their future life of bondage.

On the balcony along with us, stood three or
four slave dealers, overlooking the herd of human
victims below, and speculating upon the qualities
of each. The day was bright and beautiful, and
there was in this curious scene no appearance of
wretchedness, except what was imparted to it by
reflection from our own minds.

ORDINANCE OF NULLIFICATION OF SOUTH CAROLINA

1832

> South Carolina opposed the impo-
> sition of heavy duties on imported
> goods by the Federal Government.
> The following is the Ordinance of
> Nullification.

Source: Herman V. Ames, ed. State Documents on Federal Relations: The States and the United States. Philadelphia: Published by the Department of History of the University of Pennsylvania, 1906, 38-41

An Ordinance

To Nullify Certain Acts of the Congress of the United States, Purporting to be Laws, Laying Duties and Imposts on the Importation of Foreign Commodities.

Whereas, the Congress of the United States, by various acts, purporting to be acts laying duties and imposts on foreign imports, but in reality intended for the protection of domestic manufactures, and the giving of bounties to classes and individuals engaged in particular employments, at the expense and to the injury and oppression of other classes and individuals, and by wholly exempting from taxation certain foreign commodities, such as are not produced or manufactured in the United States, to afford a pretext for imposing higher and excessive duties on articles similar to those intended to be protected, hath exceeded its just powers under the Constitution, which confers on it no authority to afford such protection, and hath violated the true meaning and intent of the Constitution, which provides for equality in imposing the burdens of taxation upon the several States and portions of the Confederacy. *And whereas,* the said Congress, exceeding its just power to impose taxes and collect revenue for the purpose of effecting and accomplishing the specific objects and purposes which the Constitution of the United States authorizes it to effect and accomplish, hath raised and collected unnecessary revenue, for objects unauthorized by the Constitution.—

We, therefore, the People of the State of South Carolina, in Convention assembled, do Declare and Ordain, and it is hereby Declared and Ordained, That the several acts and parts of acts of the Congress of the United States, purporting to be laws for the imposing of duties and imposts on the importation of foreign commodities, and now having actual operation and effect within the United States, and more especially an act entitled "an act in alteration of the several acts imposing duties on imports," approved on the nineteenth day of May, one thousand eight hundred and twenty-eight, and also, an act entitled "an act to alter and amend the several acts imposing duties on imports," approved on the fourteenth day of July, one thousand eight hundred and thirty-two, are unauthorized by the Constitution of the United States, and violate the true meaning and intent thereof, and are null, void and no law, nor binding upon this State, its officers, or citizens; and all promises, contracts and obligations, made or entered into, or to be made or entered into, with purpose to secure the duties imposed by said acts, and all judicial proceedings which shall be hereafter had in affirmance thereof, are, and shall be held, utterly null and void.

And it is further Ordained, That it shall not be lawful for any of the constituted authorities, whether of this State, or of the United States, to enforce the payment of duties imposed by the said acts, within the limits of this State; but it shall be the duty of the Legislature to adopt such measures and pass such acts as may be necessary to give full effect to this Ordinance, and to prevent the enforcement and arrest the operation of the said acts and parts of acts of Congress of the United States within the limits of this State, from and after the first day of February next; and the duty of all other constituted authorities, and of all persons residing or being within the limits of this State, and they are hereby required and enjoined, to obey and give effect to this Ordinance, and such acts and measures of the Legislature as may be passed or adopted in obedience thereto.

And it is further Ordained, That in no case of law or equity, decided in the Courts of this State, wherein shall be drawn in question the authority of this Ordinance, or the validity of such act or acts of the Legislature as may be passed for the purpose of giving effect thereto, or the validity of the aforesaid acts of Congress, imposing duties, shall any appeal be taken or allowed to the Supreme Court of the United States; nor shall any copy of the record be permitted or allowed for that purpose; and if any such appeal shall be attempted to be taken, the Courts of this State shall proceed to execute and enforce their judgment, according to the laws and usages of the State, without reference to such attempted appeal, and the person or persons attempting to take such appeal may be dealt with as for a contempt of the Court.

And it is further Ordained, That all persons now holding any office of honor, profit or trust, civil or military, under this State, (members of the Legislature excepted) shall, within such time, and in such manner as the Legislature shall prescribe, take an oath, well and truly to obey, execute and enforce this Ordinance, and such act or acts of the Legislature as may be passed in pursuance thereof, according to the true intent and meaning of the same ; and on the neglect or omission of any person or persons so to do, his or their office or offices shall be forthwith vacated, and shall be filled up as if such person or persons were dead or had resigned ; and no person hereafter elected to any office of honor, profit or trust, civil or military, (members of the Legislature excepted) shall, until the Legislature shall otherwise provide and direct, enter on the execution of his office, or be in any respect competent to discharge the duties thereof, until he shall, in like manner, have taken a similar oath ; and no juror shall be impannelled in any of the Courts of this State, in any cause in which shall be in question this Ordinance, or any act of the Legislature passed in pursuance thereof, unless he shall first, in addition to the usual oath, have taken an oath that he will well and truly obey, execute, and enforce this Ordinance, and such act or acts of the Legislature as may be passed to carry the same into operation and effect, according to the true intent and meaning thereof.

And we, the People of South Carolina, to the end that it may be fully understood by the Government of the United States, and the people of the co-States, that we are determined to maintain this, our Ordinance and Declaration, at every hazard, *Do further Declare*, that we will not submit to the application of force, on the part of the Federal Government, to reduce this State to obedience ; but that we will consider the passage, by Congress, of any act authorizing the employment of a military or naval force against the State of South Carolina, her constituted authorities or citizens, or any act abolishing or closing the ports of this State, or any of them, or otherwise obstructing the free ingress of vessels to and from the said ports, or any other act, on the part of the Federal Government, to coerce the State, shut up her ports, destroy or harass her commerce, or to enforce the acts hereby declared to be null and void, otherwise than through the civil tribunals of the country, as inconsistent with the longer continuance of South Carolina in the Union ; and that the People of this State will thenceforth hold themselves absolved from all further obligation to maintain or preserve their political connexion with the people of the other States, and will forthwith proceed to organize a separate Government, and to do all other acts and things which sovereign and independent States may of right do.

SLAVERY ON A SOUTH CAROLINA PLANTATION

The following is a brief view of
slavery in South Carolina during
the ante-bellum era by a British
traveller.

Source: Allan Nevins, comp. and ed. American Social
History as Recorded by British Travellers. New
York: Henry Holt & Co., 1923, 154-156.

It appears that when the negroes go to the field in the morning,
it is the custom to leave such children behind, as are too young
to work. Accordingly, we found a sober old matron in charge
of three dozen shining urchins, collected together in a house near
the centre of the [slave] village. Over the fire hung a large pot
of hominy, a preparation of Indian corn, making ready for the
little folks' supper, and a very merry, happy-looking party they
seemed. The parents and such children as are old enough to be
useful, go out to work at daybreak, taking their dinner with them
to eat on the ground. They have another meal towards the close
of day after coming home. Generally, also, they manage to cook
up a breakfast; but this must be provided by themselves, out of
their own earnings, during those hours which it is the custom,
in all plantations, to allow the negroes to work on their own
account.

It was pleasant to hear that, in most parts of the country, the
negroes of America had the whole of Sunday allowed them, excepting, as I afterwards learnt, at certain seasons of the year, and in
certain sections of Louisiana; for example, where sugar is culti-
vated, it is occasionally of such consequence to use expedition,
that no cessation of labor is permitted. Generally speaking, the
planters, who seem well aware of the advantage of not exacting too
much service from their slaves, consider the intermission of one
day, at the least, as a source rather of profit than of loss. A
special task for each slave is accordingly pointed out daily by the
overseer; and as soon as this is completed in a proper manner, the
laborer may go home to work at his own piece of ground, or tend
his pigs and poultry, or play with his children—in a word, to do as
he pleases. The assigned task is sometimes got over by two o'clock
in the day, though this is rare, as the work generally lasts till
four or five o'clock. I often saw gangs of negroes at work till
sunset.

We went into several of the cottages, which were uncommonly
neat and comfortable, and might have shamed those of many
countries I have seen. Each hut was divided into small rooms
or compartments, fitted with regular bed places; besides which,
they had all chimneys and doors, and some, though only a few of

them, possessed the luxury of windows. I counted twenty-eight huts, occupied by one hundred and forty souls, or about five in each. This number included sixty children.

On returning to dinner, we found everything in perfect order. The goodness of the attendance in this house, together with the comfort, cleanliness, and cheerfulness of the whole establishment, satisfied me, that by a proper course of discipline, slaves may be made good servants—a fact of which, I confess, I had begun to question the possibility. Regularity in arrangement—good sense and good temper—an exact knowledge of what ought to be done, with sufficient determination of character to enforce punctual obedience, are requisites, I suspect, more indispensably necessary in slave countries, than in places where the service is voluntary.

It will easily be understood, indeed, that one of the greatest practical evils of slavery, arises from persons who have no command over themselves, being placed, without any control, in command of others. Hence passion, without system, must very often take the place of patience and method; and the lash—that prompt, but terrible, instrument of power—and one so dangerous in irresponsible hands—cuts all the Gordian knots of this difficulty, and, right or wrong, forces obedience by the stern agony of fear, the lowest of all motives to action. The consequence, I believe, invariably is, that where service is thus, as it were, beaten out of men, the very minimum of work, in the long run, is obtained. Judicious slave-holders, therefore, whether they be humane persons or not, generally discover, sooner or later, that the best policy by far, is to treat these unfortunate dependents with as much kindness as the nature of the discipline will allow.

The gentlemen of the South sometimes assert, that the slave population are rather happier than the labouring classes in the northern parts of their own Union, and much better off than the peasantry of England. There is no good purpose served by advancing such pretensions. They are apt to excite irritation, sometimes ridicule; and while they retard the cause of improvement, substantiate nothing in the argument, except the loss of temper. It signifies little to talk of the poor laws of England, or the pauperism in the great cities on the American coast; for, after all, such allusions apply to a small portion only of the labouring classes; whereas, in a slaveholding country, the whole working population are included in this humiliating description. . . . Have not ignorance, irreligion, falsehood, dishonesty in dealing, and laziness, become nearly as characteristic of the slave, as the colour of his skin? And when these caste marks, as they may almost be called, are common to the whole mass of the labouring population of the States in question, it is certainly not quite fair to place them on a level with the free New Englanders of America, or the bold peasantry of Great Britain.

SOUTH CAROLINA IN THE 1850'S

Frederika Bremer visited the United States during the 1850's and
presented interesting descriptions of the areas she toured.
The following excerpt is a
view of various parts of South
Carolina.

Source: Adolph B. Benson, ed. America of the Fifties:
    Letters of Frederika Bremer. New York: The Ameri-
    can-Scandinavian Foundation, 1924.

Columbia, South Carolina, May 25. The
voyage up the Savannah River, which I had been
warned against as slow and monotonous, was more
agreeable than I can tell. The weather was charm-
ing, and as the stream was strong and the river
swollen from the spring floods, the voyage was
slow; I had plenty of time to observe the banks
between which the river wound, and though mile
after mile and hour after hour presented me with
only one scene, yet this scene was *primeval forest.*
Masses of foliage from innumerable trees and
shrubs and beautiful climbing plants seemed rest-
ing upon the water on each side of the river, the
shores of Georgia and Carolina. Lofty, deep and
impenetrable extended the primeval forest—as I
was told, for many miles inland.

But here it existed in its original luxuriance and
splendor. I seemed to myself to be present on the
third day of creation, when God called forth the
vegetable world, "every tree whose seed was in
itself after his kind." On the day when the earth
opened its maternal breast and produced all the
various trees and flowers of the earth, Savannah,
with its red-brown water, was a river newly sprung
from chaos and rich with its essence, nor yet had
had time to settle itself and clear its water when
the green plants of earth sprang forth in wild
luxuriance; it seemed to play with them, and they,

newly upsprung from the water, seemed to have
no wish to part from it, but half longed to fall
back into it. Flower-laden climbing plants flung
themselves to the very tops of the trees, and then
fell down to dip again in the waves of the river.
From amid these masses of verdure, forming
porticoes, pyramids, and the most fantastic and
massive creations, glanced forth, now and then,
a catalpa, all flaming with its yellowish-white
flowers; dark-green, solemn magnolias lifted up
their snow-white blossoms toward the light, beautiful and pure as it. I noticed sycamores, amber-
bearing poplars, tulip trees with their splendid
yellow and red flecked blossoms, mulberries, many
kinds of oak, elms, and willows as I went along,
and high above all towered cypresses, with their
long, depending mosses, spreading their vast
arms abroad, like patriarchs over the low tribes
of vegetation. Not a human dwelling was to be
seen on these shores, not a trace of human activity.
There was neither the sight nor sound of animal
life, and although alligators are numerous in the
Savannah River, I did not see one; not a bird sang,
and all was silent and hushed, even the wind itself.
It was a desolation full of fantastic beauty, and just
now in the pride of its splendor. At length I saw,
sitting on the naked boughs of a dead fir-tree, two
large birds of prey, reminding the beholder that
"death was come into the world."

Thus we sped on, in a high-pressure boat, the
Oregon, with its two reeking chimneys, up the
river, mile after mile, hour after hour, while the
morning and the evening, the sun and the moon,
seemed to contend which should most beautify the
scene. And I sang in my soul, as the earliest colonists of Georgia had done before me, "How beautiful is creation, how glorious the Creator!" and
then I thought, what a poem, what a glorious
romance is this portion of the world in its natural
life; what wealth, what beauty, what varied scenes
it embraces in its bosom! I was now again alone
with America; America revealed her mysteries to

me and made me aware of her wealth, the inheritance of future generations.

The voyage was an incessant feast for me, and I wished only to be silent and enjoy it. But in order to do that, I had to avoid, in the saloon, a throng of handsome but noisy young girls who had made, on their own account, a pleasure-party and now ran about here and there, chattering, calling to one another, and laughing; and on deck, a few gentlemen, planters, who were polite and wished to talk, but talked only of "cotton, cotton, cotton," and how the world was beginning to busy itself about American cotton. I fled away from these worshipers of cotton, and endeavored to be alone with the river and the primeval forest and with the light and shadows within it. There was with the troop of young girls also a youth, a handsome man, a brother or relative of some of them. Later on in the evening he had to leave the vessel, and then the noisy young girls took hold of him, embraced and kissed him, the one after the other, in fun and amid laughter, while he, half annoyed and half amused, endeavored to get loose from them. What impression would that young man carry away with him of that night's scene? Not esteem for woman. One of the elder gentlemen on deck shook his head at the young girls' behavior. "They make a fool of that young man!" said he to me. It was not till late in the night that I could get to sleep for the noise which these girls made.

The next day was Sunday, and life seemed to celebrate a holy day, so still and so festively adorned appeared all nature. The noisy young girls had become quiet, and assembled before the door of my cabin, which was open toward the river. They were evidently in a state of mind to hear something serious. The peace of the Sabbath rested upon them. Had now some sower, commissioned of Heaven, sown the seed of truth and the comprehension of the higher life in the souls of these young girls, the seed would

assuredly have fallen in good ground. I have
faith in the inborn pure earnestness of woman's
nature and its kinship with the highest spiritual
life, and it grieved me when I saw it running wild
as in this case. Not that I think a moment of wild-
ness is of much consequence in a human life; all
depends upon the main direction of the whole.
But if nature is left to itself, it becomes a wilder-
ness, and wildernesses of human nature are very
much less beautiful than those of the primeval
forest—nor would even these be good to live in.
The spirit of a superior nature must lay his hand
upon the young heathen before he can become full
of human dignity and beauty. . . .

The slave villages in Georgia have the same
exterior as those in Carolina, and the condition
of the slaves on the plantations seem to me similar
also. The good and the bad masters make the
only difference; but then, in such circumstances,
this is immeasurable.

"Here lives the owner of a plantation who is
universally known as cruel to his people," was
once said to me as I went past a beautiful country
house almost concealed by thick trees and shrubs.
People know this, and they do not willingly hold
intercourse with such a man, that is all. Neither
the angel of justice nor of love ventures into these
mystical groves, where human beings are sacri-
ficed. What paganism amid Christianity! But
this avenges itself, nevertheless, on the white
races, as is evident in many things.

When recently at home with a Mr. Bones, I
heard the negroes singing. I wished rather to
have heard their own naïve songs, but was told
that they "dwelt with the Lord," and sang only
hymns. I am sorry for this exclusiveness; nevertheless, their hymns sung in quartette were glorious. It would be impossible to have more exqui-
site or better singing. They had hymn-books before them, and seemed to be singing from them;
but my friends laughed, doubting whether they
were for actual use. In the midst of the singing a
cock began to crow in the house, and kept on

crowing incessantly. From the amusement this occasioned, I saw that there was more in it than appeared. Nor was it, in reality, a cock that crowed, but a young negro from a neighboring court, who, being possessed of the cock's ability to crow, chose to make one in the concert.

After this, another young negro, who was not so evangelical as the rest, came and sang with his banjo several of the negro songs universally known and sung in the South by the negro people, whose product they are, and in the Northern States by persons of all classes, because they are extremely popular. The music of these songs is melodious, naïve, and full of rhythmical life and the deepest, tenderest sentiment. Many of the songs remind me of Haydn's and Mozart's simple, artless melodies; for example, "Rosa Lee," "Oh, Susannah," "Dearest May," "Carry Me Back to Old Virginny," "Uncle Ned," and "Mary Blane," all of which are full of the most touching pathos, both in words and melody. The words, however, are frequently inferior to the music; they are often childish, and contain many repetitions both of phrases and imagery; but frequently, amid all this, expressions and turns of thought which are in the highest degree poetical, and with bold and happy transitions, such as we find in the oldest songs of our Northern people. These negro songs are also not uncommonly ballads, or, more properly, little romances, which contain descriptions of their love affairs and their simple life's fate. There is no imagination, no gloomy background, rich with saga or legend, as in our songs; but, on the other hand, much sentiment, and a naïve and often humorous seizing upon the moment and its circumstances. These songs have been made on the road; during the journeyings of the slaves; upon the rivers, as they paddled their canoes along or steered the raft down the stream; and, in particular, at the corn-huskings, which are to the negroes what the harvest-home is to our peasants, and at which they sing impromptu whatever is

uppermost in their hearts or in their brain. Yes,
all these songs are peculiarly improvisations, which
have taken root in the mind of the people,
and are listened to and sung to the whites, who,
possessed of a knowledge of music, have caught
and noted them down. And this improvisation
goes forward every day. People hear new songs
continually; they are the offspring of nature and of
accident, produced from the joys and the sorrows
of a child-like race. The rhyme comes as it may,
sometimes clumsily, sometimes no rhyme at all,
sometimes most wonderfully fresh and perfect;
the rhythm is excellent, and the descriptions have
local coloring and distinctiveness. Alabama,
Louisiana, Tennessee, Carolina, "Old Virginny,"
all the melodious names of the Southern States and
places there, the abodes of the slaves, are intro-
duced into their songs, as well as their love histo-
ries, and give a local interest and coloring not
only to the song, but to the state and to the place
which they sing about. Thus these songs are like
flowers and fragrance from the negro life in those
states—like flowers cast upon the waves of the
river, and borne hither and thither by the wind—
like fragrance from the flowers of the wilder-
ness in their summer life, because there is no
bitterness, no gloomy spirit in these songs. They
are the offspring of life's summer day, and bear
witness to this. And if bitterness and the condition
of slavery were to cease forever in the free land
of the United States, these songs would still live,
and bear witness to the light of life, even as the
phosphorescent beam of the fire-fly shines, though
the glow-worm may be crushed. . . .

I here became acquainted with a German, Professor Lieber, an author of talent, and a worthy
man. For the rest there was nothing very remark-
able here, unless it were the great number of
colonels. All gentlemen of wealth, planters or
others, it matters not, are called colonel, though
they may not have been military. Such colonels
abound in the Southern States. When I expressed
my astonishment at this general promotion, I was

told that when the President of the United States
visited the various states he nominated many of
these gentlemen to be his adjutants for the
occasion; and these adopted and have since re-
tained the title of colonel. Imagine that title for
so small service! The passion for titles
which evidently distinguishes a portion of the
republican people of America, especially in the
South, is a little possessed of the devil, and but
little in harmony with the aim of this community.
The old Adam in the old uniform is going about
still.

Charleston, June 10. In South Carolina the
spirit and the links of social life are aristocratic to
a degree which I cannot approve of, however
much I may like certain people there. And aristoc-
racy there has this in common with aristocracies
of the present time; that, while the aristocratic
virtues and greatness have vanished, merely the
pretension remains. The formerly rich, magnificent planters exist no longer. Wealth, power, mu-
nificent hospitality are all gone. And, bowed
beneath the yoke of slavery, the Southern States
are a long way behind those of the North in their
rapid development, in prosperity and population.
The emigration of the present day is also beginning to bring in its manufactures and mechanical
art even into the Southern States, but much more
in Georgia than Carolina. Yet even here a man
from New England, Mr. Gregg, has lately established a cotton manufactory, similar to that of
Lowell, laid out beautifully with garden-plots for
the work-people. Far behind the Northern States
stands the South in any case, as regards moral and
intellectual culture, and this in consequence of the
unhappy slave institution, with all its consequences
both to the black and the white population. There
are great individuals in the Southern States, but
no great community, no united, aspiring people.
The fetters of slavery bind, more or less, all and
every one. Yet I love the South. I have found

there many things to love—many things to esteem—many things to enjoy—many things to be
grateful for; and as it is natural to me to enter into
the life amid which I am living or observing, I have
in the South felt myself to have a Southern tendency; and having entered into the peculiar life of
the South, its circumstances and position, having
a little sense of the good which abundantly exists
here, which is here in operation, I have perfectly
understood that bitter feeling which ferments,
even in noble minds, toward the despotic and unreasonable North, against that portion of the
North which is so opposed to the South; against
the ultra-abolitionists and their violence. It is
merely when I oppose them to the ultra of the pro-
slavery party that I hold with the former. But
what would I not give if the South, the true, the
noble South, would itself take the subject of con-
tention in hand, and silence the mouth of its
opponents, silence their blame, both just and unjust, in a great and noble way, by laws which
would bring about a gradual emancipation, by
one law, at least, which should allow the slaves
to purchase their own freedom and that of their
families at a reasonable price, a price which should
be established by law. This, it seems to me,
might be required from the Southern States, as an
act of justice to themselves, to their native land—
so far as they desire to have part in its proud character of liberty, and which they do desire—as an
act of justice to their posterity, to the people whom
they have enslaved, and for whom they thereby
would open a future, first by means of hope, by a
noble object for which to strive, and then a new
existence in a life of freedom, either in Africa, or
here in their adopted country, as the free servants
or laborers of the whites; for I confess that, according to my opinion, the Southern States would
lose a great part of their charm and their peculiar
character in losing their black population. Bananas, negroes, and negro songs are the greatest
refreshments of the mind, according to my experience, which I found in the United States. And to

every one, whether in Old or New England, who is
troubled by spleen or dyspepsia, or over-excitement
of brain or nerves, I would recommend, as a rad-
ical cure, a journey to the South to eat bananas, to
see the negroes, and hear their songs. It will do
them good to go through the primeval forest, with
its flowers and its odors, and to sail upon the red
rivers! But the negroes are preferable to everything else. They are the life and the good humor
of the South. The more I see of this people, their
manners, their disposition, way of talking, of acting, of moving, the more I am convinced that they
are a distinct stock in the great human family, and
are intended to present a distinct physiognomy, a
distinct form of the old type man, and this physiognomy is the result of temperament. . . .

As regards the slave owners, I may divide them
into three classes: Mammon-worshipers, patriarchs, and heroes or men of progress. The first
regard the slaves merely from a pecuniary point
of view, and use or misuse them at pleasure. The
second consider themselves responsible for their
office; consider that they cannot and ought not
to surrender the property which they have inherited from their fathers, and which, perhaps, is all
that they possess for themselves and their children;
and they regard it as an imperative duty to preserve these inherited servants, to provide for their
old age, to make their present life as happy as possible by means of instruction and Christianity, and
to allow them as much freedom and as much innocent pleasure as possible. The third, highest class,
advances the well-being of the slaves with reference to their emancipation; and this is done by
means of education and such practical aids. They
advance both people and country on the path of
human cultivation. I have heard mention made of
some persons even in Carolina as belonging to this
latter class, and in particular of two wealthy ladies
who have lately liberated their slaves. This is for-
bidden by law; but here also public opinion has
begun to go ahead of the law; and the lawyers

themselves aid by passing statutes to this end, and
when they are reproached with this, they laugh, and
seem untroubled by conscience.

I have heard some very beautiful traits of the
patriarchs as well as of their slaves, and of the
devotion on both sides. I believe them, because
I have seen various instances of the kind, and they
appear to me very natural. There is, upon the
whole, no human being for whom I have a greater
esteem and sympathy than the good and conscien-
tious slaveholder, for his position is one of difficulty and full of trouble. . . .

One evening which I spent at Mr. Gilman's I
was present at the evening worship of the negroes,
in a hall which that good, right-thinking minister
had allowed them to use for the purpose. The first
speaker, an old negro, was obliged to give place to
another, who said he was so full of the power of
the word that he could not possibly keep silence,
and he poured forth his eloquence for a good hour,
but said the same thing over and over again.
These colored preachers were far inferior to those
whom I heard in Savannah.

Finally, he admonished one of the sisters "to
pray." On this, an elderly, sickly woman began
immediately to pray aloud, and her evident fervor
in thanksgiving for the consolation of the Gospel
of Christ, and her testimony on behalf of His
powers, in her own long- and suffering life, were
really affecting. But the prayer was too long; the
same thing was repeated too often, with an incessant thumping on the bench with her fists as an
accompaniment to every groan of prayer. At the
close of this, and when another sister was admonished to pray, the speaker added, "But make it
short, if you please!" This sister, however, did
not make it short but longer than even the first with
still more circumlocution and still more thumping on the bench. A third sister, who was admonished to pray, received the brief, definite in-
junction, "But *short*." And when she lost herself
in the long bewilderment of prayer, she was inter-
rupted without ceremony by the wordy preacher,

who could no longer keep silent, but must hear himself talk on for another good hour. Nor was it until the singing of one of the hymns composed by the negroes themselves, such as they sing in their canoes, and in which the name "Jerusalem" is often repeated, that the congregation became really alive. They sang so that it was a pleasure to hear, with all their souls and with all their bodies in unison; for their bodies rocked, their heads nodded, their feet stamped, their knees shook, their elbows and their hands beat time to the tune and the words which they sang with evident delight. One must see these people singing if one is rightly to understand their life. I have seen their imitators, the so-called "Sable Singers," who travel about the country painted up as negroes, singing negro songs in the negro manner and with negro gestures, as it is said; but nothing can be more radically unlike, for the most essential part of the resemblance fails — namely, *the life.* . . .

Of the mysteries of Charleston I shall not tell you anything because I know them not, excepting by rumor, and that which I know merely by rumor I leave untold. Dark mysteries, more indeed than rumor has told, cannot fail in a great city in which slavery abides. I have heard it said that there is a flogging institution in Charleston for slaves, which brings the city a yearly revenue of more than ten thousand dollars. Every person who wishes to have his slave punished by the whip sends him there with money for his chastisement. I have both heard and read of this many times, and I believe it to be true. But the position of things here makes it difficult, nay, next to impossible, for me to search into such things. And I cannot and will not become a spy. I receive merely that which comes to me compulsively by my own experience, and which I therefore consider as a knowledge by higher design, as a something which I ought to know and to receive. I have here properly to do with the ideal and to cease and present it purely and faithfully. And it is in the feeling of that ideal South, as it already exists in some degree, and as it sometime may wholly exist in order to fulfill the design of the Creator, that I now bid farewell to the South with both admiration and love—sorrowing for that which it now is not, and hoping again to return.

THE SIEGE AND CAPTURE OF FORT SUMTER

Source: America. Great Crises in Our History Told By
Its Makers. Chicago: Americanization Department,
Veterans of Foreign Wars of the United States, 1925.

THE SIEGE AND CAPTURE OF FORT SUMTER

By Major John Gray Foster

MAJOR FOSTER (later brevetted major-general) assisted Major Robert Anderson in the defense of Fort Sumter, April 12-13, 1861, when it was bombarded and reduced by the Confederate batteries in Charleston Harbor. As director of engineering operations of the United States troops at Charleston, Foster had superintended the construction of Fort Sumter and the repairing of Fort Moultrie, from which he had helped transfer the Federal garrison to Fort Sumter. He was a graduate of West Point.

On April 11, 1861, acting under orders from President Jefferson Davis, General Beauregard, commanding the Confederate forces at Charleston, had demanded the evacuation of the fort. Anderson refused to withdraw. The historic bombardment followed, as here recounted. The garrison of 128 men left the fort on April thirteenth with the honors of war. There was no one wounded or killed on either side during the action.

APRIL 12th—At one a.m. four aides of General Beauregard . . . came with a second letter, stating that as Major Anderson had been understood to make a remark to the bearers of the first letter, in taking leave, that he would "await the first shot, and if not battered to pieces, would be starved out in a few days," it was desired to know what importance might be attached to it. The reply of Major Anderson did not satisfy the aides, who were authorized in that case to give notice that the fire would open. Accordingly, on leaving at 3:30 a.m., they gave notice that their batteries would open in one hour.

At 4:30 a.m. a signal shell was thrown from the mortar battery on James Island; after which the fire soon became general from all the hostile batteries. . . .

At 7 a.m. the guns of Fort Sumter replied, the first shot being fired from the battery at the right gorge angle, in charge of Captain Doubleday. . . .

The supply of cartridges, 700 in number, with which the engagement commenced, became so much reduced by the middle of the day, although the six needles in the fort were kept steadily employed, that the firing was forced to slacken, and to be confined to six guns—two firing towards Morris Island, two towards Fort Moultrie, and two towards the batteries on the west end of Sullivan's Island.

At 1 o'clock two United States men-of-war were seen off the bar, and soon after a third appeared.

The fire of our batteries continued steadily until dark. The effect of the fire was not very good, owing to the insufficient caliber of the guns for the long range, and not much damage appeared to be done to any of the batteries, except those of Fort Moultrie, where our two 42-pounders appeared to have silenced one gun for a time, to have injured the embrasures considerably, riddled the barracks and quarters, and torn three holes through their flag. . . .

The effect of the enemy's fire upon Fort Sumter during the day was very marked in respect to the vertical fire. This was so well directed and so well sustained that from the seventeen mortars engaged in firing 10-inch shells, one-half of the shells came within or exploded above the parapet of the fort, and only about ten buried themselves in the soft earth of the parade without exploding. In consequence of this precision of vertical fire, Major Anderson decided not to man the upper tier of guns, as by doing so the loss of men, notwithstanding the traverses and bomb-proof shelters that I had constructed, must have been great. . . .

. . . The effect of the direct fire from the enemy's guns was not so marked as the vertical. For several hours firing from the commencement a large proportion of their shot missed the fort. Subsequently it improved, and did considerable damage to the roof and upper story of the barracks and quarters, and to the tops of the chimneys on the gorge. . . .

The night was very stormy, with high wind and tide. I found out, however, by personal inspection, that the exterior of the work was not damaged to any considerable extent, and that all the facilities for taking in supplies, in case they arrived, were as complete as circumstances would admit. The enemy threw shells every ten or fifteen minutes during the night. The making of cartridge bags was continued by the men, under Lieutenant Meade's directions, until 12 o'clock, when they were ordered to stop by Major Anderson. To obtain materials for the bags all the extra clothing of the companies was cut up, and all coarse paper and extra hospital sheets used.

April 13.—At daybreak no material alteration was observed in the enemy's batteries. The three U. S. men-of-war were still off the bar. The last of the rice was cooked this morning, and served with the pork —the only other article of food left in the engineer mess-room, where the whole command has messed since the opening of the fire. After this the fire was reopened, and continued very briskly as long as the increased supply of cartridges lasted. The enemy reopened fire at daylight, and continued it with rapidity. The aim of the enemy's gunners was better than yesterday. . . .

It soon became evident that they were firing hot shot from a large number of their guns, especially from those in Fort Moultrie, and at nine o'clock I saw volumes of smoke issuing from the roof of the officers' quarters, where a shot had just penetrated. From the exposed position it was utterly impossible to extinguish the flames, and I therefore immediately notified the commanding officer of the fact, and obtained his permission to remove as much powder from the magazine as was possible before the flames, which were only one set of quarters distant, should encircle the magazine and make it necessary to close it. All the men and officers not engaged at the guns worked rapidly and zealously at this, but so rapid was the spread of the flames that only fifty barrels of powder could be taken out and distributed around in the casemates before the fire and heat made it necessary to close the magazine doors and pack earth against them. The men then withdrew to the casemates on the faces of the fort. As soon as the flames and smoke burst from the roof of the quarters the enemy's batteries redoubled the rapidity of their firing, firing red-hot shot from most of their guns. The whole range of officers' quarters was soon in flames. The wind being from the southward, communicated fire to the roof of the barracks, and this being aided by the hot shot constantly lodging there, spread to the entire roofs of both barracks, so that by twelve o'clock all the woodwork of quarters and of upper story of barracks was in flames. Although the floors of the barracks were fire-proof, the utmost exertions of the officers and men were often required to prevent the fire communicating down the stairways, and from the exterior, to the doors, window frames, and other woodwork of the east barrack, in which the officers and men had taken their quarters. All the woodwork in the west barrack was burned. The clouds of smoke and cinders which were sent into the casemates by the wind set on fire many boxes, beds, and other articles belonging to the men, and made it dangerous to retain the powder which had been saved from the magazine. The commanding officer accordingly gave orders to have all but five barrels thrown out of the embrasures into the water, which was done.

The small stock of cartridges now only allowed a gun to be fired at intervals of ten minutes. . . .

At 1 o'clock the flagstaff, having been struck twice before this morning, fell. The flag was immediately secured by Lieutenant Hall, and as soon as it could be attached to a temporary staff, hoisted again upon the parapet at the middle of the right face by Lieutenant Snyder, Corps of Engineers, assisted by Hart, and Davey, a laborer.

About this time information was brought to the commanding officer that Mr. Wigfall, bearing a white flag, was on the outside, and wished to see him. He accordingly went out to meet Mr. Wigfall, passing through the blazing gateway, accompanied by Lieutenant Snyder. In the meantime, however, Mr. Wigfall had passed to an embrasure on the left flank, where, upon showing the white flag upon his sword, he was permitted to enter, and Lieutenant Snyder entering immediately after, accompanied him down the batteries to where some other officers were posted, to whom Mr. Wigfall commenced to address himself, to the effect that he came from General Beauregard to desire that, inasmuch as the flag of the fort was shot down, a fire raging in the quarters, and the garrison in a great strait, hostilities be suspended, and the white flag raised for this object. He was replied to that our flag was again hoisted on the parapet, that the white flag would not be hoisted except by order of the commanding officer, and that his own batteries should set the example of suspending fire. He then referred to the fact of the batteries on Cummings Point, from which he came, having stopped firing, and asked that his own white flag might be waved to indicate to the batteries on Sullivan's Island to cease also. This was refused; but he was permitted to wave the white flag himself, getting into an embrasure for this purpose. Having done this for a few moments, Lieutenant Davis, First Artillery, permitted a corporal to relieve him. Very soon, however, a shot striking very near to the embrasure, the corporal jumped inside, and declared to Mr. Wigfall that "he would not hold his flag, for it was not respected."

At this moment the commanding officer, having reentered through an embrasure, came up. To him Mr. Wigfall addressed nearly the same remarks that he had used on entering, adding some complimentary things about the manner in which the defense had been made, and ending by renewing the request to suspend hostilities in order to arrange terms of evacuation. The commanding officer desiring to know what terms he came to offer, Mr. Wigfall replied, "Any terms that you may desire—your own terms— the precise nature of which General Beauregard will arrange with you."

The commanding officer then accepted the conditions, saying that the terms he accepted were those proposed by General Beauregard on the 11th, namely: To evacuate the fort with his command, taking arms and all private and company property, saluting the United States flag as it was lowered, and being conveyed, if he desired it, to any Northern port. With this understanding Mr. Wigfall left, and the white flag was raised and the United States flag lowered by order of the commanding officer.

Very soon after a boat arrived from the city, containing three aides of General Beauregard, with a message to the effect that, observing the white flag hoisted, General B. sent to inquire what aid he could lend in extinguishing the flames, &c. Being made acquainted with the condition of affairs and Mr. Wigfall's visit, they stated that the latter, although an aid of General Beauregard, had not seen him for two days.

The commanding officer then stated that the United States flag would be raised again, but yielded to the request of the aides for time to report to their chief and obtain his instructions. They soon returned, with the approval of all the conditions desired except the saluting of the flag as it was lowered, and this exception was subsequently removed after correspondence. In the morning communication was had with the fleet, and Captain Gillis paid a visit to the fort.

The evacuation was completed after saluting the flag, in doing which one man was instantly killed, one mortally and four severely wounded, by the premature discharge of a gun and explosion of a pile of cartridges. . . .

BASIC FACTS

Capital City .... Columbia

Nickname .... The Palmetto State

Flower .... Carolina Jessamine

Bird .... Carolina Wren

Tree .... Palmetto

Song .... *Carolina*

Stone .... Blue Granite

Entered the Union .... May 23, 1788

STATISTICS*

Land Area (square miles) 30,225
    Rank in Nation 40th

Population† 2,688,000
    Rank in Nation 26th
    Density per square mile 88.9

Number of Representatives in Congress 6

Capital City .... Columbia
    Population 113,542
    Rank in State 1st

Largest City .... Columbia
    Population 113,542

Number of Cities over 10,000 Population 18

Number of Counties 46

---

* Based on 1970 census statistics compiled by the Bureau
of the Census.
† Estimated by Bureau of the Census for July 1, 1972.

SOUTH CAROLINA

MAP OF CONGRESSIONAL DISTRICTS

OF SOUTH CAROLINA

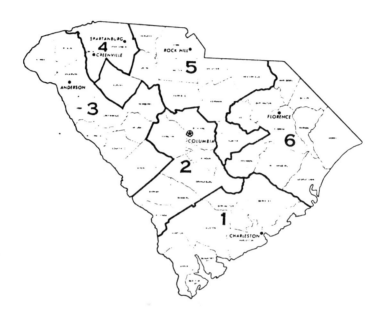

SELECTED BIBLIOGRAPHY

Cooper, William James. The Conservative Regime: South
    Carolina, 1877-1890. Baltimore: The Johns Hopkins
    Press, 1968.

Easterby, James Harold. Guide to the Study and Reading
    of South Carolina History. Columbia, S. C.: His-
    torical Commission of South Carolina, 1949-50. 2
    vols.

Lander, Ernest McPherson. A History of South Carolina,
    1865-1960. Columbia: University of South Carolina
    Press, 1970.

Hennig, Mrs. Helen Kohn. Great South Carolinians.
    Chapel Hill: The University of North Carolina
    Press, 1940-49. 2 vols.

McCants, Elliott Crayton. History, Stories and Legends
    of South Carolina. Dallas, Texas: The Southern
    Publishing Company, 1927.

Meriwether, Robert Lee. The Expansion of South Caro-
    lina, 1729-65. Kingsport, Tenn.: Southern Pub-
    lishers, Inc., 1940.

Oliphant, Mary C. Simms. The New Simms History of
    South Carolina. Columbus, S. C.: The State Com-
    pany, 1940.

Rhett, Robert Goodwyn. Charleston; An Epic of Carolina.
    Richmond, Va.: Garrett and Massie, Inc., 1940.

Sirmans, Marion Eugene. Colonial South Carolina: A
    Political History, 1663-1763. Chapel Hill: Pub-
    lished for the Institute of Early American History
    and Culture at Williamsburg, Va., by the Univer-
    sity of North Carolina Press, 1966.

Smith, William Roy. South Carolina as a Royal Pro-
    vince. New York: The Macmillan Company, 1903.

Snowden, Yates, ed. History of South Carolina. Chicago
    and New York: The Lewis Publishing Company, 1920.
    5 vols.

Taylor, Rosser Howard. Ante-Bellum South Carolina: A
    Social and Cultural History. Chapel Hill: The
    University of North Carolina Press, 1942.

Wallace, David Duncan. South Carolina, Short History,
    1520-1948. Chapel Hill: University of North Caro-
    lina Press, 1951.

NAME INDEX

145

146   SOUTH CAROLINA

Harley, Joseph E., 23, 24
Harper, William, 15
Harry, Peter, 10
Harvey, Wilson G., 23
Hayne, Robert Y., 13
Heyward, Duncan C., 21
Hollings, Ernest F., 25

Jackson, Andrew, 6, 21
James II, King of England, formerly Duke of York, 9
Jasper, William, 22
Jeffries, R. M., 24
Jeter, Thomas D., 19
Johnson, Andrew, 17, 18
Johnson, Sir Nathaniel, 3
Johnson, Robert, 4
Johnston, Olin D., 23

Kyrle, Richard, 2

Laurens, Henry, 7, 9
Lee, Robert Edward, 21
Lincoln, Abraham, 7
Locke, John, 1
Lowndes, Rawlins, 7
Ludwell, Philip, 3
Lynch, Thomas, 6
Lyttleton, William Henry, 5

Madison, James, 11
Manning, John, 15
Manning, Richard I., 22
Manning, Richard J., 12
Marion, Francis, 9
Marlborough, John Churchill, Duke of, 9
Matthews, John, 8
Maybank, Burret R., 23
McCormick, Cyrus Hall, 22
McDuffie, George, 13
McGrath, Andrew G., 17
McLeod, Thomas G., 23
McNair, Robert E., 26
McSweeney, Miles B., 21

Middleton, Arthur, 4
Middleton, Henry, 11
Miller, Stephen D., 12
Montague, Lord Charles Greville, 6
Moore, James, 3
Moore, James, 4
Moses, Franklin J., Jr., 18
Morton, Joseph, 2
Moultrie, William, 9, 10

Nixon, Richard M., 27
Noble, Patrick, 13

Orr, James L., 17

Perry, Benjamin F., 17
Pickens, Andrew, 7, 11, 12
Pickens, Francis W., 16
Pinckney, C., 16
Pinckney, Charles, 9, 10, 11
Pinckney, Thomas, 9
Poinsett, Joel R., 13

Quarry, Robert, 2

Ribaut, Jean, 1
Richards, John G., 23
Richardson, James B., 10
Richardson, John P., 19
Roosevelt, Franklin D., 23
Roper, Daniel C., 23
Russell, Donald S., 26
Rutledge, Edward, 10
Rutledge, John, 6, 7

Sayle, William, 1
Scott, Robert K., 18
Sheppard, John C., 19
Sherman, General, 17
Simms, William Gilmore, 15
Simpson, William D., 19
Smith, Charles A., 22
Smith, Thomas, 3
Southell, Seth, 2
Sumner, Charles, 15